INTERPRETING DEVELOPMENT

John Girling

INTERPRETING DEVELOPMENT

CAPITALISM, DEMOCRACY, AND THE MIDDLE CLASS IN THAILAND

STUDIES ON SOUTHEAST ASIA

Southeast Asia Program
Cornell University, Ithaca, New York
1996

Cornell Southeast Asia Program Publications
640 Stewart Avenue, Ithaca, NY 14853-3857

Studies on Southeast Asia No. 21

Printed in the United States of America

ISBN 0-87727-720-6

CONTENTS

Acknowledgements   7

Preface   9

Major Events from 1947   11

1. Interpreting Development: The Problematic of Capitalism and Democracy   13

2. Thailand: The Four Contradictions   19
     Rapid, but Uneven, Development   19
     Military Assertion   25
     Business Power   31
     Money Politics   35
     The Range of Business-Political Relations   40

3. The Middle Class and Civil Society   43
     Middle Class and Alternatives   43
     Civil Society and the Role of NGOs   61

4. Twin Peaks—Disturbing Shadows   77
     Economics, Politics, Society in the 1990s   77

5. Conclusion: Development and Democracy Reconsidered   93

ACKNOWLEDGEMENTS

I benefited greatly, during a recent short visit to Thailand, from reading books and discussing ideas with Pasuk Phongpaichit and Chris Baker; with Ammar Siamwalla and Scott Christensen; and with Prudhisan Jumbala and his colleagues. I gladly acknowledge, too, correspondence with Anek Laothamatas and the opportunity to meet, at conferences, with Chai-Anan Samudavanija and Kasian Tejapira. I am no less grateful for the extensive comments and advice, especially of Kevin Hewison, and of Benedict Anderson, Benedict Kerkvliet, Rapin Quinn (for her inspiring work on NGOs), Julaporn Euarukskul, and Pierre Fistié.

Particular thanks go to Rick Doner for his most perceptive critique, making me re-think the focus of this study. Such is the best kind of critic-author symbiosis! And my thanks, too, for the continuing interest and concern shown by Audrey Kahin, at that time managing editor of the Southeast Asia Program Publications of Cornell University, and of her successor, Deborah Homsher, in making publication possible.

I am most grateful to the late director of the Institute of Southeast Asian Studies, Kernial Sandhu, who invited me for a year's fellowship to work on Thailand, and to the next director, Chan Heng Chee, the then deputy director, Sharon Siddique, and the executive secretary, Y. L. Lee. I acknowledge, with pleasure, the friendship and intellectual stimulus of scholars such as Yao Souchou, Diana Wong, and Surin Maisrikrod; and, indeed, of many others.

PREFACE

I was quite actively engaged in analyzing—and at times experiencing—economic, political, and social changes in Thailand during the 1960s and 1970s. But in the next decade I was concerned, more generally, with theories of society and development.

What I have attempted to do, in the present work, is to capitalize on the "assets" of this particular form of intellectual transition—from the concrete to the abstract, from empirical analysis to theories and models—and minimize the "debits" (separation from substantial work on Thailand during a decade of significant change).

The first task of research is to consider the major factors contributing to economic growth, the evolution of state power, the emergence of civil society, and so on. The second task is to evaluate the relationship between these factors as well as their relationship to the "whole" (the society in question). The analysis of Thai society thus reveals: in economic terms, the ascendancy of capitalist development; in political terms, the spasmodic reaction of formerly dominant elements of the "bureaucratic polity," especially the military, on the one hand, and the convulsive emergence, at times of crisis, of civil society, on the other; finally, in cultural or symbolic terms, the changing status of élites, the commercialization of values, and renewed drives for legitimacy.

In one sense, economic and political developments go together, contributing to a more open, democratic society. In another sense, the economic opportunities proliferating under capitalism (both legal and illegal) also make possible an upsurge in vote-buying and election funding, as well as ministerial abuse of public office for private gain; in other words, capitalistic opportunism undermines the still precarious institutions of democracy.

Despite these impediments, civil society in Thailand plays a significant role as a forum for professionals, political parties, the media, unionists, and other intermediate elements, seeking autonomy from the state and to a varying extent from the economic system.

The viewpoint of civil society is expressed in the (citizens') ideology of democracy, seen as universal and transcendental, and presupposing the innate dignity of every person. The counterpart to the ideology of civil society is the (rightwing) ideology of nationalism, which invokes historic triumphs or current ambitions, emphasizing the "security" of the nation and the designated instrument of that security (the military). Finally, there is the ideology of "development," justifying the ascendancy of capitalism and the political role of the middle class, which forms the third element in the triangular relationship between economic growth, state power, and civil society. The complex interaction of these ideas and practices is the subject of this work.

MAJOR EVENTS

From 1947

1947   Military coup. Civilian leader Pridi in exile

1948–57   Marshal Phibun era: Police-gen. Phao–Gen. Sarit rivalry. Restrictions on (Chinese) business. Sarit's coup, 1957

1958–63   Martial law; "national development," technocratic planning; bureaucrat-business partnerships

1963–73   Generals Thanom and Prapart rule: corruption and repression; parliamentary interlude (1969–71). Industrialization, banking, infrastructure

1973   Victory of student-led constitutional movement (October); "tyrants" exiled. Communists active ("people's war" from 1965)

1973–76   Democratic period: conservative Kukrit, Seni governments. Student turbulence (rightist violence)

1976   Military coup: Thanin installed. Radical students join communist insurgency

1977   Military coup: pragmatic Kriangsak government; constitution drafted

1980   Prem government: support of Young Turks

1981   Young Turks coup fails (and in 1985)

1980s   "Premocracy" (to 1988): coalition governments (usually Democrat, Chart Thai, Kukrit's SAP); business people in parliament, cabinet, provinces; bureaucrat-business consultation

1984   Baht devalued (economic recession) despite military opposition. From mid-1980s, foreign investment flows; accumulation of domestic capital; economic policy reforms

1987   Chamlong elected Governor of Bangkok

1988–91   Chatichai Government: Politicians benefit from economic boom, corruption charges. Chavalit forms New Aspiration Party. Reduction in military budget: confrontation with "Class 5"

1991   Suchinda's coup (February): Anand's reforming administration; military-dictated constitution

1992   Military-backed parties win elections (March); Suchinda reneges on promise not to become prime minister. Protest demonstrations (May) led by Chamlong, Confederation for Democracy, fired on by troops. Stock–market collapse. King intervenes. Anand governs (June). Elections (September). Chuan (Democrat) government

1993   Abolition of military "peacekeeping" act (June)

1994   Chuan coalition changes (December)

1995   Land reform scandal: defection of Palang Dharma: "vote-buying" elections (July): Chart Thai coalition

1

INTERPRETING DEVELOPMENT: THE PROBLEMATIC OF CAPITALISM AND DEMOCRACY

Following the dramatic transition to democracy (with a market economy) in Latin America, Eastern Europe, and East Asia, a transition greeted with enthusiastic welcome around the world, there is now a widespread tendency to assume that "development" is economic growth and that the combination of "development" and "democracy," once established, is a lasting panacea for social ills.

This inspirational approach, however understandable, neglects a number of important questions. One wants to ask what are the implications of capitalist development? And what kind of democracy is emerging? For democracy is no more static, fixed in time and space, than development (obviously). Indeed, the very concept of "democratization" implies a process of social interaction—a process that reflects the ever-changing balance of forces in society.

Even the assumed priority of economic growth obscures awkward aspects of current development. In Eastern Europe, for example, the "shock treatment" of the changeover from planned to market economy has resulted in substantial social dislocation (and deprivation) followed, in certain countries, by the equally "shocking" return to power of reformed ex-communists.

The problematic status of development and democracy reflects the inadequacy of a purely political concept of democracy—where political equality conceals economic inequality—and the inadequacy of a purely economic concept of development —where even the material benefits provided by an authoritarian regime, for example, are no substitute for loss of civil and political rights.

Consider again, in this respect, the truly remarkable transition to "development and democracy" described above. There has been a redistribution of political power (from authoritarian regimes) especially to the growing middle class; yet there has been no similar redistribution of economic control or wealth, but rather the reverse, the enlargement and concentration of economic power. Moreover, one important result of the "transition" has been the emergence or revival of a "political class," composed of leading and usually conservative members of civil society, who are best able to "manage" the political accommodation with capitalism required by the process of "development."

Such a result, which appears to be the case in such diverse countries as Mexico and Brazil, Poland and the Czech Republic, Singapore and Thailand, raises the crucial question of the relationship between capitalism and democracy. Historically, it is of great significance that the foundation of democracy, as in the United States and France, and the establishment of the parliamentary regime (as in Britain), *preceded* the ascendancy of capitalism, thus helping to preserve democratic institutions and values against the encroachments of capitalism.

But even in these birthplaces of democracy, the impact of capitalism—as the eminent and by no means radical sociologist Max Weber recognized—has been immense. Two major developments affecting political behavior, especially in the last half century, have been the importance of electoral funding and the spread (through advertising, television, etc.) of commercialized values. Above all, there has emerged a consensus among leading politicians, regardless of party, on the overriding need to improve competition (in an increasingly global economy) and to maintain business confidence.

If such is the case in the most economically and politically advanced nations, how much greater is the impact of domestic (and international) capitalism on the fragile political systems of "developing" countries? Yet the situation is not as clear-cut as it might seem. For in many of these countries capitalism is itself only an "emerging" and far from fully established force. (The "non-success" stories in large areas of Africa, the uneven developments in Latin America, and the crises of the Philippines under Marcos, or Indonesia under Sukarno, make the point.)

Moreover, the historical relationship between "pre-modern" or colonial regimes and emerging capitalism is ambiguous. Such regimes often developed certain capitalist sectors—usually in order to gain more revenue—but at the same time they sought to preserve "traditional" sectors (such as small-holder agriculture and artisanal enterprise) for the sake of social stability. These constraints on capitalist development remain an important feature of the contemporary world.

Nevertheless, the general trend of modern development, and particularly with regard to the "success stories" in East and Southeast Asia—such as Korea, Taiwan, Malaysia and Thailand—has been to weaken such institutional restraints, imposed by previously powerful bureaucracies, in favor of greater freedom for capitalist expansion and the play of market forces.

REGIONAL PERSPECTIVE

A useful way to illustrate the problematic of development and democracy—that is, the range of possibilities, including setbacks as well as progress, open to such countries—is to consider it in regional perspective. In East Asia, for example, Japan is seen as "the economic leader and most established democracy," while the "Newly Industrializing Economies" [NIEs], such as "democratizing" Korea and Taiwan, are at the next level, followed by "quasi-democratic" countries like Malaysia and Thailand "still feeling the tug of authoritarianism," with the "less-developed, more authoritarian regimes" at the end of the line. Yet each country experiences pressures "to push it up to the echelon ahead."[1]

---

[1] Harold Crouch and James W. Morley, "The Dynamics of Political Change," in James W. Morley (ed.), *Driven by Growth: Political Change in the Asia-Pacific Region* (New York: M.E. Sharpe with Columbia University, 1993), p. 278. See also Ruth McVey (ed.), *Southeast Asian Capitalists* (Ithaca, New York: Cornell University, Studies on Southeast Asia, 1992), especially her sparkling introduction, "The Materialization of the Southeast Asian Entrepreneurs." As she emphasizes: "It is at the level of major industries that we find most clearly displayed the nexus of business, politics, and the state . . . central to the Southeast Asian capitalist upsurge," p. 9; see also pp. 13–14, 30–32. Also important is the discussion in Kevin Hewison, Richard Robison, and Garry Rodan (eds.), *Southeast Asia in the 1990s: Authoritarianism, Democracy and Capitalism* (Sydney: Allen & Unwin, 1993).

Japan is the role model. For Japan's own history indicates the course that other countries in the region are taking. In the first half of this century, Japan started at the lowest level (as Vietnam does now). It was an exporter of simple, cheaply made consumer goods, especially textiles. It was a country with a large, oppressed, and poor rural population. Last, it was a country under the rule of a powerful authoritarian state, where civil society, with its democratizing potential, was either barely tolerated or ruthlessly suppressed.[2]

At the present time, of course, Japan is a world economic power, challenging or surpassing its Western rivals. The military is constitutionally subordinate to the democratically elected government and, while the influence of bureaucrats remains substantial, the bureaucracy has reached a consensus with big business and the ruling politicians to give priority to economic growth.

At the second level, South Korea and Taiwan are no longer low-wage economies, with predominant agricultural sectors, but are urbanized and (via strong state support) "newly industrialized" nations. The authoritarian regimes in countries at this "second level" are increasingly being eroded, as civil society provides the impetus for ever more effective measures of democratization: putting an end to martial law, legalizing the political process, establishing a free press.

At the third level are countries like Thailand, Malaysia, and the Philippines, where capitalism is emergent, where the structure of the state reflects the impact of economic and social changes (resulting, ambiguously, in both the contestation and the assertion of state power), and where civil society is increasingly vocal.

At the fourth level are low-wage economies like Indonesia and Vietnam, which remain under authoritarian rule, but which face challenges from members of civil society (especially academics, lawyers, journalists, and religious leaders) on behalf of human rights, press freedom, environmental concerns, and economic and social reforms.

Viewed from this evolutionary perspective, Thailand's development is instructive. In Thailand, sustained economic growth for more than three decades has been accompanied by the rise of business from its original "dependent" status to one of virtual equality (if not superiority) with the military and civilian administrators in power and esteem. Significantly, a major role of the state itself (from the era of the military dictator, Sarit, onwards) has been to facilitate capitalist development, by rationalizing the bureaucratic machinery of decision making, introducing economic incentives, and encouraging foreign investment. Moreover, the very process of economic development has resulted in the growth of civil society (notably, professionals, organizers, and intellectuals) seeking a voice in the formation of public policy.

Thailand represents an intermediate stage in the evolutionary process: it is no longer a "bureaucratic polity" (society dominated by the military in an informal partnership with big business), but it is not yet a "bourgeois polity"—capitalism with democracy—as in Japan.

---

[2] "Civil society" includes professionals, managers, academics and students, media persons, members of non-governmental organizations (environmentalists, feminists, consumer representatives, rural development workers, and so on), members of religious groups and civic associations, labor leaders and unionists, peasant organizers and activists. Each member has his or her occupational or class interest, but also a view of the general interest. They are united as *citizens*.

How can this empirical process be theorized? Two major theories of social development which might be used are Marxism (and its variants) and what was formerly known as "Modernization theory." Both are theories of stages of development—one judges progression through these stages in terms of conflict (class struggle), the other in terms of civic cooperation. The two theories propose entirely different, although equally predetermined, outcomes.

Orthodox Marxism posits the inevitable collapse of capitalism as it reaches maturity, a collapse which results due to its inherent contradictions: economic contradictions, because of private appropriation of the social product of the workers engaged in production; and social contradictions, in class terms, because of the antagonism between the desperate mass of exploited proletarians—by now in alliance with a ruined middle and lower middle class—and the ruthless minority of wealthy capitalists. According to the Marxist schema, now discredited by events, the revolution of the masses against capitalism ushers in a classless society, which distributes justly (according to people's needs) an increasingly abundant product.

Modernization theory, to the contrary, proclaims the stage-by-stage development of the productive process, which is reflected socially in the "progress" of the middle class, accompanied by the domestication of the "responsible" elements of the working class, both of which in time overcome the pre-capitalist "traditional" obstacles to change. Indeed, economic and political changes occur in tandem, creating capitalism with democracy—a market economy with political freedom—according to the Western model.

Neither Marxism nor Modernization theory, however, has been able to explain substantial deviations from the predicted process. Nevertheless, the recent inspiring transformations in Latin America and Eastern Europe have given Modernization theory a new lease of life. Samuel Huntington's influential "Third Wave" approach to democratization as an end-product of economic development reflects these changes. As Huntington puts it, "economic development—industrialization, expansion of literacy and education, urbanization, increased wealth, decreasing inequalities in income and wealth, the emergence of a bourgeoisie and a middle class—has generally played a critical role [in democratization]." Further, "the spread of Western ideas of liberal democracy to other societies and the expansion of the power of the West have also been centrally important in the expansion of democracy to non-Western societies."[3]

Huntington, however, assumes a direct political transition (to democracy) as a result of economic development. He tends to ignore the crucial importance—in Eastern Europe as in Latin America—of the "intermediary" role of civil society in relation to the economy and the state. Against Huntington's interpretation, I would argue that three evolving situations, which gradually lead to the replacement of an authoritarian leadership by a more liberal government, must characterize a country in order for it to make the transition to democracy. These characteristics are the

---

[3] Samuel P. Huntington, "Democracy: Its Evolution and Implementation" for conference on Asian and American Perspectives on Capitalism and Democracy, Singapore, January 1993. See also Samuel P. Huntington, *The Third Wave: Democratization in the Late Twentieth Century* (Norman, Okla.: University of Oklahoma Press, 1991). The first democratic wave came in the nineteenth century, then receded; the second in the 1960s, ditto; the "third wave" is from the 1980s. Despite the more sophisticated empirical explanation of the transition from authoritarianism to democracy in this book (e.g. pp. 141-42, 169), Huntington still concludes by equating economic development and democracy: p. 311.

bankruptcy of the authoritarian state; the growth of a mature civil society, from which a new political leadership could emerge; and the implicit bargain by which the displaced authoritarian leaders and cadres generally escape prosecution or reprisals in return for their (temporary, in some cases) retirement from the political scene.

These three characteristics, which are no less relevant to social transformation in the East Asian region, provide a more satisfactory explanation than does Huntington's "wave" theory of the ambiguities in the capitalism-democracy nexus. Indeed, such characteristics help to explain the erosion of the authoritarian power-structure in South Korea and Taiwan from the mid-1980s and the subsequent process of democratization. Yet the state is still powerful in both countries, and the "old guard"—backed by "traditional" ideas and norms—continues to pose a formidable obstacle to the realization of liberal democracy.

In Southeast Asia, the recent history of the Philippines is a reminder of the fragility of formally democratic institutions (which lack a representative social content) in the face of powerful and ambitious political and military leaders. Nor does the authoritarian record of the Indonesian "New Order" inspire confidence in any "automatic" transition to democracy once a certain level of economic development has been reached. Even in Thailand, despite remarkable progress toward a more open society, the military coup of February 1991 followed by the bloody events of May 1992 indicate how real the threat of authoritarianism remains.

It is precisely because of these ambiguities—the conflictual as well as the cooperative tendencies in the interaction of economy, state, and civil society—that I propose "four contradictions" (rather than Huntington's "third wave") as essential elements in a theoretical scheme to be used for analyzing "development" in Thailand. The four contradictions are: the rise of business; the assertion as well as contestation of state (particularly military) power; the role of "money politics"—the deviant expression of capitalism—in undermining democratization; and the growing importance, despite the above impediments, of civil society.

I call them "contradictions," not because these political and economic entities, directed by leaders with different interests, have proven incapable of cooperating with one another (indeed, business and authoritarian leaders have often worked together), but because each element is essentially autonomous—a "driving force" of its own. The present role of business, discussed in chapter two, is far greater than that of early "pariah" capitalism, which was dependent on state patronage and protection, for business now has the capacity and the will to act independently—to form an alliance with military leaders, at a particular conjuncture, or with civil society, in furthering democratic institutions, when the time seems right.

Similarly, the "fixers" in the provinces who mobilize electoral support or buy votes (in return for favors from the politicians they have elected) also play a significant and often constructive role in mediating between government officials and villagers, in local entrepreneurial activities, and as patrons providing goods and services to "their" voters. The fixers may choose between these different concerns and some have even become politicians themselves; or they can move out of illegal deals into legitimate business.

Military leaders, too, face different options. Basically, they have to decide whether to keep up their "old guard" tradition of direct intervention in politics, however discredited by the events of May 1992, or work out new and more sophisticated ways of influencing political decisions. But a military decision to abandon its leadership claims and return to the barracks, in keeping with democratization, cannot simply be assumed inevitable.

Further, as will be evident from chapter three—on the middle class and civil society—even members of civil society have to decide among conflicting tendencies. They are united as "citizens" against an overbearing state, but in their occupational or class categories, as middle class professionals or as artisans, small business people, and workers, they have different and often contradictory interests in relation to capitalism and the state. The empirical interaction of these varying tendencies is examined in chapter four. The outcome is problematic; so is the relationship (reconsidered in chapter five) between development and democracy.

2

THAILAND: THE FOUR CONTRADICTIONS

RAPID, BUT UNEVEN, DEVELOPMENT

(i) REVOLUTIONS AND REVERSALS

Where Vietnam is now, in many ways, Thailand was in the early postwar years. It was ruled by an authoritarian regime; it had a limited economy, exporting rice and other unprocessed products, and a predominantly rural population; business was headed by ethnic Chinese family firms, thriving economically, but politically dependent on an informal partnership with military-political faction chiefs; and civil society barely existed.

The remarkable change, over the past thirty years, to the present financial and manufacturing economy, semi-democracy, and intermittently influential civil society, occurred, not through a Huntington-style cyclical wave of democratization, but as a result of three "revolutions"—economic, political, and societal—followed in the last two cases by major setbacks.

The first revolution was economic. This was Sarit's turnaround in the early 1960s, repudiating economic nationalism (and its promotion of the public sector) and instead mobilizing state resources, through the development of infrastructure and encouragement of foreign investment, to serve the private sector. The resulting economic boom, with cyclical adjustments, continues to this day, radically transforming Thai society. As a prime example, the contribution of agriculture to gross domestic product has halved from some 30 percent in 1970 to 12 percent today. Conversely, manufacturing and financial and other services are now dominant. At the same time, the overwhelming proportion of the Thai population living in the countryside has not greatly declined (from eight out of every ten to about two out of three). The "drag" of a rural lifestyle retards, in the social and political spheres, the impact of economic modernization. This, as will be seen, is a major impediment to fuller democracy.

The second revolution erupted as a political turning point: the student-led demonstrations of the early 1970s, which confronted the discredited military-dominated regime of Sarit's factionalized successors. The heroic stand by students, formerly conservative and careerist, but now representing the conscience of the nation, directly contributed to the downfall of the leading military-political clique.

The ensuing, premature, "democratic period" in effect signaled the end of the "bureaucratic polity": that is, the hegemony of military and civilian officials who divided political appointments (and distributed wealth) among themselves. For half a century, leaders in the bureaucracy had dominated the elements outside the bureaucracy—apart from the mutually advantageous "partnership" with important

Sino-Thai business concerns. But most political and social groups were powerless or dependent: these included interest groups (incipient and largely personalized), political parties (the same), the few professionals, a passive religious establishment, the controlled media, and so on.

The successful student defiance of the bureaucratic leadership in 1973 thus marked a turning point, not so much structurally (for the military remained powerful), but in a symbolic sense. Hitherto, when the military had asserted its "right to rule," usually by staging a coup against the formal institutions of democracy, there was little or nothing that citizens could do—or think of doing—about the fait accompli. The existing constitution (following the fate of countless predecessors) was simply abrogated, the parliament dissolved, political parties (and trade unions where permitted) were banned, and the country placed under martial law. Citizens were dependent upon the military and civilian bureaucracy; their inactivity at times of crisis was an implicit recognition of their dependency. The constitutionalist demonstration of 1973 marked the end of that phase. No longer would military pressures, threats, or intervention remain uncontested.

The third revolution, in contrast to the turbulence of the 1970s, denotes the emergence of civil society. "Premocracy" (the coalition governments under prime minister and former army commander Prem during most of the 1980s) relied on the countervailing power of political parties, largely supported—and financed—by business, and the growth of professional associations and interest groups, which were intricately balanced by General Prem, himself under royal favor, with market-oriented technocrats and a variety of military factions. So well institutionalized had this new political arrangement seemed to have become, as election was followed by peaceful election, that both academic and public opinion became convinced that continued progress to democracy—Huntington's "third wave"—was irreversible.

Indeed, the very replacement of General Prem by the elected politician Chatichai as prime minister in 1988 appeared only to confirm the diagnosis. This was true at least until February 1991, when a more unified military leadership staged its successful coup. Paradoxically, the 1991 coup, which disbanded the elected government, demonstrated not the revival of the bureaucratic polity but its last spasms. For it was the military leaders' brutal attempt to suppress peaceful protesters, in May 1992, that exposed the military—and not civil society—as the divisive factor in Thailand. This is an extraordinary turnaround from the time when the military's claim to be the guardian of national unity—against civilian dissidents—was widely accepted.

From that point on, too, the middle class (however heterogeneous or amorphous), the real victor of the May events, could no longer be excluded from political decision making. It is around the middle class, and particularly business interests, that the political system now revolves. So important is this turning point in Thailand's history that it is worth considering these events in more detail.

(ii) 1991–1992

The erratic political process over the last two decades, during which time Thailand's government has shifted from bureaucratic polity to bureaucratic polity via apparent democratization, illuminates the rather unpredictable interaction of "the four contradictions": that is to say, civil society, money politics, military assertion, and business power. For civil society had become increasingly influential, and was basic to the constitutional system ("Premocracy" or "semi-democracy"). But this political process was tarnished by "money politics," not simply as a result of the ever greater role of businessmen in political parties, and in government, but even more as a result of evident corruption at all stages—from the electoral activities of political candidates buying votes, especially in the countryside, to the self-serving decisions of cabinet ministers who abused public office for private gain.

Meanwhile, the military establishment, badly factionalized since the 1970s, had developed by the late 1980s a new unity around the leading group of fellow graduates of the military academy (Class 5), headed by the army commander, General Suchinda. Thwarted in previous attempts to maintain leverage over parliament, notably through control of the appointed Senate, the military seized the opportunity offered by mounting public disgust with the Chatichai government to launch its 1991 coup. Encouraged by the approval of business and the urban elite (and with the tacit support of the monarchy), the military counted on reinstituting its hegemonic command over political and civil society.

Thus, in an uncanny throwback to the Sarit era, amid accusations by the coup leaders of the Chatichai government's corruption and subversion, the existing constitution was abrogated, parliament was dissolved, and martial law was declared. On this occasion, however, the evidence of corruption was so blatant that the public—alienated by the excesses of "unusually wealthy" cabinet ministers—gave little show of support for the fallen regime. Indeed, many in business and the professions openly approved of the coup. Their attitude seemed to be all the more justified when a non-elected, technocratic government was installed by the military under an able former diplomat turned business leader. For the Anand "caretaker" government proved to be not only relatively independent of its sponsor, but was remarkably effective in pushing through long overdue policy reforms.

The first part of the game plan was successful. A constitution designed by the military was pushed through without serious difficulties; the Anand caretaker government was set up to hold the stage until suitable preparations could be made for the military's candidates to win the elections; and powerful military leaders, or their proxies, created or manipulated the major political parties, some of which were newly established, while others derived from the recent past, and one even from the "heroic" period of the 1970s. With substantial funds at their disposal and the help of "dark influences" in the provinces, the military-backed parties did win the April 1992 elections. It was at this point, with the reawakening of civil society and the beginning of doubts by business, that the military's plan began to unravel.

Allegations of drug trafficking (of all things!) doomed the prime ministerial bid by the nominal leader of the military-backed parties; corruption, evidently, was not confined to one side of politics. Then, as part of a presumed master plan, General Suchinda was appointed prime minister—reneging on an earlier promise that as an unelected official he would not enter politics. In angry reaction, in May 1992, the non-military parties, strongly supported by the public, staged massive demonstrations headed by Chamlong, charismatic former governor of Bangkok, ex-military "Young Turk," and an ardent Buddhist.

Against the backdrop of intense public excitement, Chamlong's struggle against Suchinda took on the form of a cosmic drama involving the forces of good against evil. (Indeed, "angels" were to fight "devils" in the next election.) In more mundane terms, Suchinda's reactivation of the military's "right to rule" confronted popular insistence on constitutional rule—with deadly results. Suchinda and his clique were determined to suppress opposition at all costs. Troops firing on peaceful protesters caused such carnage, and public outrage, that the king was at last compelled to intervene. In a replay of October 1973, amid growing signs of business unease (the stock exchange, sensitive as always to "disturbance," had sunk to a new low), Suchinda was obliged to resign, a caretaker government was installed (under Anand), and new elections were held. The result was a narrow victory by the democratic parties.[1]

(iii) Uneven Development: Implications for Democracy

Evidently during the 1991–1992 crisis, the four interacting contradictions met and, in certain ways, canceled and skewed one another's powers. Civil society, with its essential character demonstrated by the middle-class and urban composition of the anti-military protest movement, has triumphed, but its victory is precarious. Military leaders have suffered a severe setback, but the military as institution is still largely beyond parliamentary control. Business "confidence"—both domestic and international—was a crucial ingredient in the resolution of the May 1992 crisis, but business power was insufficient to prevent the crisis occurring in the first place. Finally money politics, although of lesser effect in city elections, is still rampant in the countryside, where the majority of people live.

With its last spasm in May 1992, the bureaucratic polity is finished; but the "bourgeois polity" has yet to establish its hegemony. It is as if each "contradiction" has reached its peak—the military with its February 1991 coup, money politics in the March 1992 elections, and civil society in the great May demonstration, followed by the September 1992 elections—only to fall back exhausted. Only business power—especially the export-oriented economy—continues its relentless upward trend.

Thus, the present situation remains problematic. The military is no longer able to impose its own image on Thai society, but it is still a wild card. Even if the top personalities have been displaced, its national security ideology has hardly been affected. Military intimidation—threats of a coup if military interests feel themselves

---

[1] See the perceptive account by Surin Maisrikrod, "Thailand 1992: Repression and Return of Democracy," *Southeast Asian Affairs 1993* (Singapore: Institute of Southeast Asian Studies, 1993), pp. 327–43. But note Saneh Chamarik's reminder, not long after the May events and the formation of the Chuan government, that even an elected government does not guarantee "genuine democracy"—"government of the people, by the people, and for the people" in Lincoln's celebrated phrase—so long as economic policy is in the hands of technocrats and capitalists, at the expense of human rights and popular freedom: Saneh Chamarik, *Prachatipatai: rawaeng rubbaeb kab neuha* [Democracy: between form and content], *Warasan Thammasat*, vol. 19, no. 1, Jan.–April 1993, pp. 19–20. See also the thoughtful discussion by Khien Theerawit, *Wikridkan kan muang thai: karani pharispha mahawipyok 2535* [Thai political crisis: the tragic event of May 1992] (Bangkok: Matichon press, 1992), on the opposition's perception of Suchinda as illegitimate for reneging on his promise, and his acceptance of proven corrupt ministers; and the differing motivations of those opposing Suchinda: pp. 32–43, 51–57. See also Voravidh Charoenlert, "The Middle Class and May 1992" (in Thai) in Sungsidh Piriyarangsan and Pasuk Phongpaichit (eds.), *Chonchun klang bonkrasae prachathipatai thai* [The middle class and Thai democracy] (Bangkok: Political Economy Centre, Chulalongkorn University, 1993), on the role of students, workers, intellectuals, political parties, with an analysis of those killed: pp. 117–26; and Thanet Apornsuwan, "State and Thai politics in the 1990s" (in Thai) in Pasuk Phongpaichit and Sungsidh Piriyarangsan (eds.), *Rat thun jao pho thongthin kab sangkhom thai* [State, capitalists, local mafia and Thai society] (Bangkok: Political Economy Centre, Chulalongkorn University, 1992), on the impact of the 1991 coup on politics, and the military attempt to restore the old order of bureaucratic control: pp. 198–200, 223–25, 232–33.

under pressure—can still disrupt established political processes and distort economic development.

Even the rise of business is double-edged. On the one hand, the more professional, metropolitan-based financial, trading, and industrial concerns have developed international linkages, establishing their own rules and norms, and maintaining institutional ties with government and bureaucracy. On the other hand, provincial business, in the context of "primitive accumulation," is more free-wheeling, personalized, and at the same time intimately linked with the new "democratizing" political process, which involves the electoral funding of favored candidates in return for public contracts, licenses, and other concessions.

Even the remarkable rate of growth of the economy in the late 1980s and early 1990s (with exports increasing twice in value since 1985) has distracted attention from underlying, long-term problems. "If the domestic issues of education [providing work skills], infrastructure, the environment, over-concentration, and excessive urbanization [Bangkok] are not dealt with, then growth could slow down significantly."[2]

The most serious obstacle to technological progress, as these economists point out, is the "acute shortage" of technically skilled secondary school graduates. Thailand's enrollment rates are twenty-five years behind those of Taiwan, and well behind even those of Indonesia and the Philippines.[3] (Only 32 percent of children of the appropriate age group are enrolled in secondary schools in Thailand, compared with 45 percent in Indonesia.)[4]

Now, facing the prospects of competition from lower-wage countries like China and Vietnam,[5] Thailand needs especially to upgrade its manufacturing base. Hence it has become important to improve labor productivity, through education and training, thus allowing more skill-intensive industries to emerge and to compete on international markets. "Even more important," as one economist argues, "improved access to education will permit the growth of a large, professional and managerial middle class which will have both the confidence and the capacity to develop new products and new markets."[6]

---

[2] Narongchai Akrasanee, David Dapice, and Frank Flatters, *Thailand's Export-led Growth: Retrospect and Prospects* (Bangkok: Thailand Development Research Institute, 1991), pp. 2, 5–6.

[3] Ibid., p. xvi.

[4] Anne Booth, "The Rising Challenge to ASEAN from the Rest of Asia," paper for International Conference on Southeast Asia: Challenges of the 21st Century (Singapore: Institute of Southeast Asian Studies, 1993), pp. 15, 24, table 5. Through the 1990s, as another specialist observes, Thailand will suffer from a severe "brain shortage" because of the defects in the education system: especially the high drop-out rate after primary school and the tendency, unusual in developing countries, of university students to choose arts courses rather than science and engineering: John Andrews, *The Asian Challenge* (Hong Kong: Longman, 1991), p. 76. Currently, Thailand produces some 3,500 engineering graduates a year—about half the industrial need: *The Economist*, reprinted *Straits Times*, May 19, 1993. The Banharn government in 1995 pledged to continue the Chuan government's emphasis on education—in particular by extending from six to nine (and then twelve) years of compulsory schooling, but the problem of shortages of teachers, textbooks, and schools remains.

[5] Labor costs in the textile industry range from more than $3 per hour in South Korea, to $1 per hour in Thailand and Malaysia, and under 50c. in China and Indonesia—and about half that in Vietnam: *The Economist*, July 31, 1993.

[6] Booth, "Rising Challenge," p. 18. See also Sompop Manarangsan, "Alternatives for Agricultural Labor" (in Thai), in Pasuk Phongpaichit and Sungsidh Piriyarangsan (eds.), *Ponlawat thai: mummong jak sethasat kanmuong* [Thai dynamics: a political-economy view]

Shortcomings in education policy, in other words, are hampering the emergence of the "bourgeois polity" predicated as part of the Western, or indeed the East Asian, model. Such shortcomings, evident in the neglect of rural secondary education, are of course the obverse side of official emphasis on Bangkok—the political, administrative, financial, and manufacturing center of the country. Such lopsided development, creating strains in the capital itself (severe pollution, traffic congestion, slum conditions), is more than an economic problem, although the slowdown in agriculture is symptomatic of distorted priorities.[7] It is also a social problem: average incomes per head in the large Northeastern region, for example, are one-fifteenth of those in Bangkok.[8]

Thus, even the transformative effect of sustained economic growth has certain built-in limitations, noted particularly in agriculture, which contributes only 12 percent of gross domestic product, yet provides nearly two-thirds of all jobs. The "drag" of the rural areas on social progress—for in these areas one finds persistent pockets of poverty, inadequate access to education, and the drift to the urban "informal economy"[9]—make it unlikely that Thailand will readily catch up with "model" countries like South Korea or Taiwan.[10]

(Bangkok: Political Economy Centre, Chulalongkorn University, 1991), on the problem of those who cannot continue secondary education (about two-thirds of those twelve to fourteen years old) and especially in the Northeast: p. 86. Currently, however, both bureaucracy and government are committed to expand education, including the secondary level: interview with Ammar Siamwalla, Director of the Thai Development Research Institute, January 14, 1994.

[7] The rate of agricultural growth has slowed from 4.2 percent in the 1970s to 3.7 percent in the first half of the 1980s and only 1.9 percent (barely keeping up with population growth) in the later 1980s. Further, the collapse of agricultural prices from the mid-1980s and their projected long-run decrease could have a harmful effect on income distribution with increase in poverty: Narongchai, Dapice, Flatters, *Export-led Growth*, pp. xv, 25–26. Crop prices have slumped from their peak in the mid-1970s, according to another study, while the end of the "land frontier" has resulted in cultivation of marginal land and erosion of forest areas. The forest cover has been halved since 1961; this is also the effect of illegal logging: Sompop Manurangsan, "Wayouts for Laborers in the Thai Agricultural Sectors," in Chira Hongladarom and Shigeru Itoga (eds.), *Human Resources Development Strategy in Thailand: Past, Present and Future* (Tokyo: Institute of Developing Economies, 1991), p. 115.

[8] *The Economist*, reprinted in *The Australian*, April 6, 1996; Seventh National Economic and Social Development Plan (1992–96), p. 2; National Statistical Office, 1990, on household incomes.

[9] Rural migrants, especially women and youths, are an important labor source in Thailand; but unlike South Korea, where they have become industrial workers, most in Thailand work in low-paid services or the informal sector. More than half the urban workers are classified as informal, typically working for small firms, subcontracting in textiles and ready-made garments for the retail and export trade. Their educational level is low (three-quarters have only elementary education) and they earn around the minimum wage. See Pasuk Phongpaichit, "Nu, Nit, Noi and Thailand's Informal Sector in Rapid Growth" in Chira and Itoga (eds.), *Human Resources*, pp. 90–98, 101, 103; and Pasuk Phongpaichit, "The Urban Informal Sector" in Pasuk and Itoga (eds.), *The Informal Sector in Thai Economic Development* (Tokyo: Institute of Developing Economies, 1992), pp. 1–6, 19–20, 28–29.

[10] A "high degree of state autonomy" from social classes or groups as well as bureaucratic efficiency and integrity have been crucial in the success of government-business relations in East Asia: Anek Laothamatas, *Business Associations and the New Political Economy of Thailand: From Bureaucratic Polity to Liberal Corporatism* (Boulder, Colo.: Westview, 1992), pp. 164–65. Kevin Hewison argues that the Thai state has taken "a strongly interventionist role in the economy"; while there is no single, clear path to capitalist development, he suggests—in line with the East Asian model—that "there is a distinct possibility that a more representative par-

Thailand's uneven development has its effect on the formation of civil society, a process influenced by the changing conditions of a booming economy, the distributional shortcomings (especially in the countryside and urban slums), and the vagaries of politics. The disparate members of civil society, ranging from affluent professionals to idealistic reformers and hard-pressed labor organizers, are nevertheless united as citizens in pursuit of a democratic society—all the more so when confronting the oppressive character of the bureaucratic polity and its surviving elements. But they are divided by economic interest and certain social values, the more conservative among them giving priority to economic growth and market forces, the more progressive either trying to persuade political parties to develop grassroots support or acting outside politics as pressure groups for environmental protection and for the empowerment of the poor and the oppressed.

The ambivalent character of each of the four contradictions—the military, business (in legitimate and deviant forms), and civil society—is discussed in turn. Military assertion, the rise of business, and "money politics" are considered in this chapter. The heterogeneity of civil society and the middle class, which is its main component, is analyzed in the following chapter.

Nevertheless, in their complex interaction—money politics versus civil society, and military assertion versus both business power and civil society—there are elements of renewal to be found in each sector.

MILITARY ASSERTION

The early role of the military was in the context of the bureaucratic polity, which provided a predictable outlook on society. After the crises of the 1970s, however, society no longer behaved in its traditional way; moreover, divergent factions in the military reflected the emergence of different strands in society. The 1980s, in particular, revealed the uncertain responses of military factions to rapidly changing economic and social conditions that escaped bureaucratic control. They reacted either by defying change, pressing for a return to the bureaucratic polity, as in 1991–1992, or by adopting various forms of accommodation to change, ranging from interventionist practices carried out in the old style to more sophisticated attempts to preserve the essentials of the military institution (and its money-making "privileges") from political interference or control. These, then, are the key variables:. the duration of the bureaucratic polity (its structure and mentality); unified or factionalized military leadership; and resistance or adaptation to change.

The bureaucratic polity was dominated by the military, which in turn dominated Thai society for half a century. The most direct form of intervention by the military was the coup d'état. "Once in control, the military junta tends to give first priority to the maintenance of power by advancing and protecting corporate interests." Key positions in the structure of government were filled by leading members of the coup

liamentary form of politics will emerge" in the service of capitalist interests: Hewison, *Bankers and Bureaucrats: Capital and the Role of the State in Thailand* (New Haven, Conn.: Yale University Southeast Asia Studies, 1989), p. 214. Nevertheless, South Korea—unlike Thailand—has overcome the "drag" of a large rural population. In forty years of economic development, the rural population in Korea has been reduced from 50 percent to only 20 percent in a preponderantly urban and industrialized country. See Scott Christensen, David Dollar, Ammar Siamwalla, and Pakorn Vichyanond, *The Lessons of East Asia: The Institutional and Political Underpinnings of Growth* (Washington: World Bank, 1993), pp. 5–6.

clique to assure stability. "Rivals and potential rivals are either eliminated or curtailed or both. Potential allies are co-opted and rewarded."[11]

Conversely, non-military elements of Thai society during the heyday of the bureaucratic polity—up to the early 1970s—were too weak, disunited, and "clientelized" to withstand military intervention. Instead, they sought in various ways to accommodate to the fait accompli. Even at the highest level, rather than "challenging the military's authority, the monarchy has reached a tacit agreement with the military regarding political equilibrium. . . . The civil bureaucracy is fragmented and relatively unorganized; it does not pose a serious threat to the military's power." During the years of high economic growth, there was a high degree of cooperation between soldiers and bureaucrats. As for political parties, when allowed to function [between coups], "many have been dominated by military leaders." Meanwhile, the business community in Thailand remains largely Chinese (Sino-Thai), and it has also shown itself ready to cooperate with the military. . "The military elite has participated actively in these [business] organizations . . . [thus] co-opting another potential competitor."[12]

Facilitating the penetration of bureaucratic power to all levels of society, Thai "traditional" values—those of a hierarchical system—helped to sustain the bureaucratic polity. Training in "proper" behavior—respect for elders, the educated, and persons of status and power—starts at an early age within the family, continues through the educational process, and is confirmed by the adult's contacts with officialdom. In an "authority culture" like this, the assumption of superiority underlying the confidence of the ruling elite has its necessary counterpart in the *acceptance* of inferiority by those of lower status and those who lack organized power.

Such was the institutional structure of Thai politics. The dynamics of the system, however, were driven by the incessant rivalry within the elite—the struggle for power and wealth by ambitious leaders and their followers—in the context of rapid socio-economic change. But industrialization and urbanization, the massive expansion of university education, and the training of managers and technocrats also created substantial and growing new social forces. Along with these new social forces, notably the urban middle class but also including the beginning of an organized working class as well as large numbers of migrants in the informal sector, new social values were being created. "The old attitudes of superiority and subordination, proper to a hierarchical society, are no longer seen to be just, reasonable, or even economically effective from the viewpoint of the young and enterprising, the socially aware, and the poor and dispossessed."[13]

Meanwhile, as power struggles within the military increasingly discredited its self-serving and repressive leadership, which was evidently incapable of reform, so urban opinion developed new conceptions of society, counterposing to the old order the legitimacy of a democratic constitution that would serve the interests, not of a particular clique, but those of people in general. The clash of interests and conscious-

---

[11] Somboon Suksamran, *Military Elite in Thai Politics* (Singapore: Institute of Southeast Asian Studies, 1984), Preface. The monograph provides biographical data on military officers in the legislature.

[12] David Morell and Chai-Anan Samudavanija, *Political Conflict in Thailand: Reform, Reaction, Revolution* (Cambridge, Mass.: Oelgeschlager, Gunn & Hain, 1981), p. 56.

[13] John L. S. Girling, *Thailand: Society and Politics* (Ithaca, New York: Cornell University Press, 1981), pp. 119, 121.

ness culminated in the crisis of October 1973, when students bravely defied the military. Their success not only undermined the self-confidence of the military leaders—their consciousness of power—but at the same time overcame what had hitherto crippled the new forces: their consciousness of lack of power. Thus, no matter what later attempts the military leaders might stage to reassert their "right to rule," there could be no going back to the bureaucratic polity. Military leaders retained the power to intervene, but that power was no longer unchallenged: indeed, it would be contested.

New rules of the game accordingly had to be devised for the new era of "compromise" between the bureaucracy (especially the factionalized military), political parties, and business, epitomized in the 1980s by "Premocracy." For most of this decade, the political-military interests of General Prem (with his close adviser, General Chavalit) prevailed, while the influence of the "Young Turks" sharply declined, and that of their rivals, the Class 5 graduates, began to rise.[14] Military leaders remained deeply suspicious of parliament as a rival (and inferior) institution—they were suspicious as well of business's growing power—but they had to develop more subtle ways of controlling or influencing their rivals.[15] Structurally, military leaders had inaugurated mass self-defense or self-help village organizations as a weapon against communist insurgents; these weapons could also be used as a counterweight to the electoral spread of political parties in the countryside.[16]

In ideological terms, the military could still present itself as the guardian of national security, defending the country not only against external threats but also against internal "subversion," as defined by the military.[17] In the same vein, military

---

[14] See Chai-Anan Samudavanija, Kusuma Sanitwongse, and Suchit Bunbongkan, *From Armed Suppression to Political Offensive: attitudinal transformation of Thai military officers since 1976* (Bangkok: Institute of Security and International Studies, Chulalongkorn University, 1987), on the Young Turks (with whom Chai-Anan had had close contacts), the Democratic Soldiers, and the Class 5 officers, whose presence was already being felt by the early 1980s: pp. 116, 118–20, 122.

[15] Chai-Anan observes: the Thai military and bureaucratic elites are by no means united, but they have a common negative attitude towards elected politicians: "Thailand: A Stable Semi-Democracy," in Larry Diamond, Juan J. Linz, and Seymour Martin Lipset (eds.), *Politics in Developing Countries: Comparing Experiences with Democracy* (Boulder, Colo.: Lynne Rienner, 1990), p. 305. He also quotes from a well-known political scientist, Kramol Thongdhamachart: "the bureaucratic elites often perceived political parties as the cause of national disunity"—as well as a threat to their power positions: ibid., p. 292. For an example of the military critique of social injustice attributed to the pressure and interest groups prevalent in Western parliamentary democracy, see Chai-Anan Samudavanija, *The Young Turks* (Singapore: Institute of Southeast Asian Studies, 1982), pp. 58–59.

[16] See Suchit Bunbongkarn, *The Military in Thai Politics 1981–86* (Singapore: Institute of Southeast Asian Studies, 1987), pp. 50–54, 63–65; see also Chai-Anan, "Semi-Democracy," on the competition between the military and bureaucracy on the one hand and political institutions on the other in organizing and mobilizing the masses: p. 299.

[17] The "Thai military has been assiduous, aggressive even, in promoting Thai national culture and national identity and in the process has enshrouded itself with the trappings of authenticity and legitimacy." Thus, the military and state security organs have nurtured a mentality both in the bureaucracy and social institutions that embraces the values that the military cherishes, notably national security. This "national security-national identity formation," serving military ambitions, frustrates the efforts by the middle class and business tycoons to develop democratic institutions and a laissez-faire economy: Craig J. Reynolds, "Introduction" to Reynolds (ed.), *National Identity and its Defenders: Thailand 1939–1989* (Monash, Australia: Monash University papers on Southeast Asia no. 23, 1991), pp. 28–29. On the other hand, Chai-

leaders voiced populist themes, claiming that the military was the only true defender of the interests of ordinary people against the corrupt ambitions of the politicians abetted by the greed of capitalist exploiters.[18]

The counter-insurgency doctrine (Prime Ministerial order no. 66/2523) elaborated by General Prem and his close advisers, notably General Chavalit, was intended to provide the legitimating role for the military in its social and political mission.[19] The military interest was made to appear in the general interest:

> The Government is determined to maintain strictly the nation, religion and monarchy and the democratic form of government with the King as head of state to administer the country, taking into consideration the people's welfare; harmonize the people's interests and preserve the Thai national identity; resolve economic, political, and social problems justly and peacefully; and instill in the Thais a sense of idealism, especially one which encourages the sacrifice of personal for common interest. . . . The armed forces will have as its major role the defense of the nation, the protection of national independence and democracy with the King as head of state. . . .

As for the objective of defeating communism, the doctrine advocated "political means" rather than military action. The stated aim was to eliminate social injustice and establish a "rule of conduct" assuring the "harmony of interests among people of different classes and a sacrifice of class interests for the common good." Of course, democratic movements, too, must be promoted, but vigilance was needed to avoid "confusion between democratic movements and communist movements which hide behind the banner of democracy."

Order no. 65/2525 took up the latter theme. Popular participation in political activities must be promoted (for the sake of popular sovereignty); but "Activities of pressure groups and interest groups must be regulated," including economic groups which have taken advantage of the "liberal economic system" and the "weak" state mechanisms for mobilizing resources and distributing benefits. Such "monopolist" groups, according to the doctrine, inflict "social injustice and material hardships on the people, creating conditions for [civil] war." Some of these groups have even developed "great political bargaining power." The order recommends "guidelines" to enforce the law against any "violation by business" and to "destroy monopolistic power." (This "social" message clearly reflects the influence of "Democratic Soldiers," one of the factions supporting Chavalit; but it had little appeal to the rising "Class 5," which, after backing Chavalit, turned against him in the later 1980s.)

The second group potentially subject to regulation is "the masses." Workers and farmers are "crucial" for Thailand's development, but they are also targets for competition among political groups, including the communists. To prevent this,

---

Anan, Kusuma, and Suchit emphasize the transformation in Thai military thinking, redefining its role in politics, especially as a result of the counter-insurgency campaign. The change has been from a purely military doctrine and strategy to one that combines development with security: Chai-Anan et al., *From Armed Suppression to Political Offensive*, pp. 128, 150, 169.

[18] Notably in the arguments of the "Young Turks" and of the "Democratic Soldiers," such as General Chavalit, currently a political party leader and former army commander.

[19] The order is translated in ISIS [Institute of Strategic and International Studies] Bulletin 2, no. 1 (January 1983) and reprinted in Suchit, *The Military in Thai Politics*, Appendix 2. Order no. 65/2525 was translated in the October 1982 ISIS Bulletin, reprinted by Suchit, Appendix 3.

"leadership of mass organizations should be won over to destroy the subversive power of the communists," while a political environment conducive to democracy [in the Thai style] should be encouraged.

Students—in the third place—"are a special group which has high political awareness and seeks democracy and social justice. However, because their experience is limited, they are targets for communist groups and used as a part of the united front constructed by the latter." Therefore, "correct political education" should be provided to students.

The activities of "progressive groups," fourthly, need to be "kept within bounds imposed by national security considerations." "Activities of those groups which constitute a threat to national security and the development of [Thai] democracy should be closely and continually observed and obstructed."

Finally, the mass media. To ensure that they are "constructive for democracy," those in the media who have democratic ideas—as officially defined—should be commended and given support. "The Government's mass media organizations should be used to promote democracy and counteract news which cause its destruction. News which has an adverse impact on the democratic system should be curtailed by executive as well as legal measures."

The wide scope for military intervention—in defense of "democracy"—is evident, given the identification of the latter with "nation, religion, monarchy": the traditional watchword of the old order, ever since the days of the absolute monarchy! Even more significant for gauging the generals' attitudes toward military intervention, as a respected academic specialist on the military points out, is the fact that both General Arthit (army commander during the first half of Prem's prime ministership) and General Chavalit himself have emphasized that as long as the political system is not a "perfect" democracy, the army should act as the "builder," and not just "protector," of democracy. Only when a "perfect and absolute democratic" system is established would the military revert to being merely the "guardian" of democracy.[20] It may well be, as Suchit suggests, that since a "perfect democracy" would be difficult if not impossible to attain, the army's determination to implement the official doctrine—*despite* the ending of the communist insurgency by the mid-1980s—"can be interpreted as an excuse to perpetuate its non-military role."[21]

Yet, while the theoretical scope for military intervention is virtually unlimited, the practical possibilities during the 1980s were more constrained. This was partly due to factionalism in the army (resulting in two abortive coups) but it was also because of the more assertive stance of businessmen and technocrats in shaping official policy, even to the detriment of military interests. One important instance was the devaluation of the baht in 1984, in accordance with economic rationalism, which was bitterly contested by the then army commander, Arthit. (Devaluation would sharply increase the cost of importing military hardware.) Despite an emotional

---

[20] Ibid., p. 74.

[21] Ibid., p. 75. Chai-Anan, Kusuma, and Suchit underline the military distrust of political parties, which are seen as corrupt, bent on power, self-interested, and without ideals. Since political institutions are not fit to bring about "true democracy," so the military perceives its duty to play an active political role, providing "leadership" for the sake of unity and security: *From Armed Suppression to Political Offensive*, pp. 153–55, 183.

appeal by Arthit on television, Prem (supported by the King) stood firm behind the technocrats, and Arthit was forced to back down.[22]

A second instructive case was the failure of the military leadership's pressure on parliament to extend the interim clauses of the 1978 Constitution. These clauses enabled serving bureaucrats to hold political office; they were also designed to ensure the joint jurisdiction of the military-dominated (appointed) Senate along with the elected House of Representatives over issues of national security, the palace, and economic affairs, in addition to votes of non-confidence. Again, despite an intensive military campaign in early 1983—including veiled threats of coups—to put pressure on conservative political parties, the military-backed amendment, which had aroused public opposition, narrowly failed.

It was not until Prem's withdrawal from politics in 1988 and the formation of the Chatichai government that the military could seize the opportunity to go on the offensive. By the early 1990s the coalition government, profiting from the remarkable economic boom, had become a byword for corruption. Even more importantly for the military (now united in its leadership) was the belief that the Chatichai government had deliberately adopted a confrontational attitude towards the Class 5 army leaders, one that was apparently designed to bring them under the control of a rival, the former army commander turned politician, Arthit. It was to preempt this possibility that the military staged its February 1991 coup, which was followed by Suchinda's assumption of political power a year later, as already outlined above.

But the consequence of Suchinda's failure to crush the popular protest demonstration of May 1992 was the further discrediting of the military's presumed "right to rule." This was followed by the humiliating demotion of its ringleaders by the second Anand caretaker government. Finally, in June 1993, the elected Chuan government abrogated the "Internal Peacekeeping Directorate Act" of 1976 (a highly symbolic date: the year of the coup that put an end to the first democratic period). It was under this act, which empowered the military to put down "civil unrest," that Suchinda had staged his coup in 1991—and had tried to suppress the democratic opposition in 1992.

In conclusion, the military has three options. (1) The Suchinda option of direct military intervention in traditional bureaucratic polity style. (2) The Chavalit option of influencing or manipulating politics by populist (anti-capitalist, anti-politicking) proclamations, and by supporting rural and urban mass organizations as counterweights—but even such indirect intervention poses problems for democracy. (3) The Vimol (he replaced Suchinda as army commander) option of developing a professional military institution, jealous of its privileges, but reluctant to intervene directly in politics except as a last resort.[23]

---

[22] Ibid., p. 43. See also Anek Laothamatas, "The Politics of Structural Adjustment in Thailand: A Political Explanation of Economic Success," in Andrew J. MacIntyre and Kanishka Jayasuriya (eds.) *The Dynamics of Economic Policy Reform in South-east Asia and the South-west Pacific* (Singapore: Oxford University Press, 1992), p. 41.

[23] The rather brittle relationship between the military and the political parties was revealed in November 1993 by the reaction of a senior military officer (close to the army commander-in-chief) to the proposed constitutional changes being debated in parliament. The officer claimed that reduction in the powers of the appointed (military-dominated) Senate would make another coup "unavoidable": interview, *Bangkok Post*, November 26, 1993. See also Prudhisan Jumbala, *Nation-building and Democratization in Thailand: A Political History* (Bangkok: Chulalongkorn University Social Research Institute, 1992), on military pressures in the 1980s, pp. 89, 97–101.

BUSINESS POWER

Neither the logic of capitalism nor whatever passes for the rationality of state managers is enough to guarantee business control of policy. If business wants things done, it has to swing into political action and demand it. This it does through persistent lobbying, by carefully influencing appointments to key positions in the state, and most of all through the service of an informal network of policy advisory institutions. . . . These organs furnish state officials with the general business view of things as well as more technical blueprints for desired policy.[24]

The long period of remarkable economic growth in Thailand has important political and social implications, as suggested in the quotation above. First, there is the sheer growth of business, and second, the change in society's evaluation of business, which has been transformed from ethnic "pariah" to a respected generator of wealth and power. (In this regard, business also plays an active role in politics.) Third, there has developed a close relationship, as during the 1980s, between business associations and governmental technocrats in pursuit of market-oriented reforms. And finally there are shifts in the ambiguous relationship between economic power and military power, notably the trend, with vacillations, away from business support for authoritarian regimes (at that time believed to ensure political stability) to awareness of the damaging impact of military interventions on domestic—and global—confidence in the economic system.

First, phenomenal economic growth rates, as one specialist puts it, have fundamentally changed the social landscape. The most obvious has been the rapid increase in average per capita gross national product, which more than tripled in just one decade, from $300 in 1977 to $1,200 in 1990. Life expectancy, too, has improved by some ten years since the mid-1960s, and literacy rates are more than 90 percent. Meanwhile rapid urbanization and the growth of a middle class are accompanied by "higher rates of crime, alienation, and corruption—social ills that are characteristic of urban centers."[25]

The motor of economic growth in Thailand has been the private sector, concentrated in large firms with a corporate business structure, fueled by the expansion of banking and finance capital. Almost all the large industrial concerns, as Hewison· points out, have a high degree of interlocking shareholding, and are also involved in trading and finance. Two hundred and twenty of the 1,399 largest Thai companies (measured by 1980 assets) were in the areas of banking, finance, and insurance and had total assets amounting to 70 percent of gross domestic product. (Thirty banks alone accounted for about 84 percent of that total.) Overall, banking capital is controlled by sixteen corporate and family groups, with widely varied interests in

---

[24] Sydney Plotkin, review of G. William Domhoff, *The Power Elite and the State* (New York, 1990), in *Political Science Quarterly*, Fall 1991, pp. 561–62.

[25] Clark D. Neher, *Southeast Asia in the New International Era* (Boulder, Col.: Westview, 1991), pp. 17–18. For a remarkable evocation of economic and socio-cultural transformation in Thailand—the spread of capitalism, urban lifestyles, and commercialization of values—see Benedict R. O'G. Anderson, "Introduction," in Anderson and Ruchira Mendiones (eds. and trans.), *In the Mirror: Literature and Politics in Siam in the American Era* (Bangkok: Duang Kamol, 1985). The darker side is brought out in Ben Anderson, "Murder and Progress in Modern Siam," *New Left Review*, no. 181, May–June 1990.

more than 550 enterprises. The six largest banks include the Bangkok Bank (with more than one-third of total deposits), the largest bank in Southeast Asia.[26]

In spite of the growing role of foreign and multinational enterprises in Thailand, the combined assets of domestic firms are five times as large. Thai banks, for example, owned 97 percent of the assets of the top twenty commercial banks. Even in the automobile and textile industries, where there is the largest foreign concentration, some 44–45 percent are owned by local businessmen. The majority of these ethnic Chinese businessmen, as Anek underlines, have adopted Thai family names, acquired Thai citizenship, and received a Thai education. Moreover, about three-quarters of business leaders (in the top 890 firms) are college graduates. As further evidence of assimilation, while children of businessmen constitute about one-third of the bureaucratic elite, conversely, increasing numbers of children of bureaucrats have become business executives in major corporations.[27]

A parallel trend, secondly, has been the shift in the social evaluation of business. "Business leadership has moved from the position of being pariah entrepreneurs," as a well-known Thai resource economist puts it, "to one that is near the center stage in politics in recent years." The early relationship was a patron-client one, with the army generals as patrons providing "protection," while the protected Chinese businessmen did well for themselves by exploiting the various monopoly powers granted them by the generals for their mutual benefit. The "democratic period" of the early 1970s was the real turning point. Bankers and industrialists "began to feel more secure about their right to hold on to their wealth," while politicians (as well as generals) needed money: "coups and elections cost a great deal of money."[28]

As a result, between 1983 and 1988 there were more than three times as many parliamentarians with business backgrounds as there were with bureaucratic careers. Nearly half Prem's cabinet ministers were businessmen. Such changes also confirm

---

[26] Hewison, *Bankers and Bureaucrats*, pp. 128, 160, 162–63, 171, 181–82, 192. For another excellent overview—of Thai political economy—see Pasuk Phongpaichit and Chris Baker, *Thailand: Economy and Politics*, chapters on" Jao Sua" and "Nai Thun," and "The Military and democracy," on military business activities, and provincial business (Kuala Lumpur: Oxford University Press, 1995).

[27] Anek, *Business Associations*, pp. 77–78, also citing research by Krirkkiat Pipatseritham and Likhit Dhiravegin.

[28] Ammar Siamwalla, "An Economic Theory of Patron-Client Relationships: with some examples from Thailand," paper for Thai-European Seminar on Social Change in Contemporary Thailand, Amsterdam, May 1980. Already by the 1960s, political patronage was not as important to business expansion as access to foreign capital, advanced technology, capacity to mobilize capital funds, and market conditions: Akira Suehiro, *Capital Accumulation and Industrial Development in Thailand* (Bangkok, 1985), quoted by Ansil Ramsay, "Contemporary Thai Political Evolution" in Ramsay and Wiwat Mungkandi, *Thailand-U.S. Relations: Changing Political, Strategic, and Economic Factors* (Berkeley: University of California Institute of East Asian Studies, 1988), p. 20. (Fred Riggs's influential study, *Thailand: The Modernization of a Bureaucratic Polity* [Honolulu, 1966], had characterized the role of ethnic Chinese business at that time as one of "pariah entrepreneurship.") Anek notes the changing attitude of business toward democracy in "Chonchun klang kab kanpatana prachatipatai nai prathet thai" [the middle class and the development of democracy in Thailand], paper for Chulalongkorn University conference, November 1992: see tables, pp. 12–15, and p. 18. By the end of 1991 business has lost its faith in the military ensuring stability (during debates over the military-proposed constitution) and especially after May 1992. "The middle class anounced that it would not accept a military-led government again"; business, with its global economic linkages, came to understand that dictatorship no longer meant stability.

As a result, between 1983 and 1988 there were more than three times as many parliamentarians with business backgrounds as there were with bureaucratic careers. Nearly half Prem's cabinet ministers were businessmen. Such changes also confirm the successful integration of ethnic Chinese into Thai society. Anek quotes, for example, the president of a provincial chamber of commerce in the Northeast, who commented in 1986: "In the past, it was common to see bureaucrats as 'important' people, and merchants as 'insignificant' people. Thus, whenever problems arose, we, merchants, dared not talk to the bureaucrats. The situation has changed recently. . . ."[29] (In Anek's view, however, clientelism continues to play an important role in the provinces, because there is still a wide gap in status between officials and business leaders. It is in Bangkok, where that gap has narrowed considerably, that what are taken for patron-client relations are often actually friendship or classmate ties.)[30]

A third important factor is the relationship between business people and technocrats in promoting market-oriented reforms. Indeed, the political and social significance of modern business was further enhanced by the shift from import-substitution to export-promotion. The early import-substitution phase, as Pasuk points out, was associated with a particular coalition of interests—notably the military and associated corporate and other "protected" interests. The military, formerly so powerful, found itself in the early 1980s fighting to retain control over the process of economic policy-making in order to defend its budget against technocratic proponents of fiscal austerity and economic reform. (In addition, key military figures had acquired substantial interests in import-substituting business.)[31]

During this critical period, from the early to mid-1980s, when Thailand was suffering from the international recession (as well as increased oil prices) inflation rose while economic growth fell (and with it government revenue), and the trade imbalance grew alarmingly. Technocrats in the National Economic and Social

---

[29] Anek, *Business Associations*, p. 101. On the growing importance of provincial business, see Kevin Hewison and Maniemai Thongyou, "The New Generation of Provincial Business in Khon Kaen: Economic and Politivcal Roles": paper for sixth international conference on Thai studies, London, SOAS, 1993. For example, business people made up more than 60 percent of members of province and munipipal councils in 1990. See also Somrudee Nicro, "Thailand's NIC Democracy: Studying from General Elections," *Pacific Affairs*, vol. 66, no. 2, 1993, on the entry of new business people into politics, leading to new methods of vote-gathering in the provinces: pp. 168, 172–78.

[30] Anek, *Business Associations*, p. 105. See also Somkiat Wantana, "The Provincial Businessmen and Thai Democracy" (in Thai), in "Chonchun klang,"paper for Chulalongkorn University conference, November 1992, on their representation in parliament. Out of 360 MPs in the House of representatives after the September 1992 elections, there were 151 from business, compared to 21 bureaucrats, and 40 lawyers: pp. 196–98, and table p. 199. (See also note 35, below.)

[31] Pasuk Phongpaichit, *Technocrats, Businessmen and Generals: Democracy and Economic Policy-making in Thailand* (Nathan, Queensland: Griffith University, 1989), p. 7; there was also a strong lobby of local entrepreneurs with a vested interest in protection: pp. 11–12. (Pasuk's paper was reprinted in MacIntyre and Jayasuriya, *Dynamics of Economic Policy Reforms.*) See also Kevin Hewison, "The Financial Bourgeoisie in Thailand," *Journal of Contemporary Asia*, 11, no. 4, 1981; and Medhi Krongkaew, "Trends in the Thai Economy and Implications for Thailand's Foreign Economic Policies," in Ansil and Wiwat, *Thailand-U.S. Relations*. Theeranat Karnjana-uksorn, "The Military and Business" (in Thai), in "Chonchun klang,"paper for Chulalongkorn University conference, November 1992, draws attention to the character of the Thai military (quite different from that of the middle class) as well as to its patronage and rent-seeking activities: pp. 280–83, 288–92 (various examples).

Development Board, backed by the Prem government, pressed for a series of policy reforms to avert the danger of economic collapse. Increasingly assertive business organizations, such as the Association of Thai Industries, the Board of Trade, Thai Bankers' Association, and the Chamber of Commerce moved in the same direction, seeking formal representation on government advisory boards, direct personal contacts with important policy-makers, and the ability to exert pressure through their representatives in parliament.[32]

Against the backdrop of economic crisis, major policy reforms were carried out—including successive devaluations of the currency, gradual reduction in tariffs, tax reforms, a new credit policy, and export promotion. The economy was reoriented into a new phase of export-led growth. It responded dramatically to these changes. The GNP growth rate doubled to more than 8 percent from 1986 to 1987 and rose even higher in subsequent years. It was accompanied by a huge increase in foreign investment, especially from Japan, but also from the European Community and the United States.

The key player in this striking transformation, Pasuk argues, was the business sector—even more so than domestic technocrats and foreign institutions. Indeed, the change has been viewed by one of the leading technocrats (also a strong proponent of government-business collaboration) as reflecting a shift from "decadent capitalism," characterized by corrupt dealing between officials and businessmen, to "mature capitalism," revealed by open consultative procedures, and above all, "government's displayed responsiveness to the legitimate requests of business representatives, and the deregulation of the economy."[33] This assessment is premature; but there is no doubt about the dynamism, if not the social "maturity," of Thai capitalism.

A more problematic issue, finally, is the relationship between business and authoritarian regimes. Changing attitudes reflect the shift from "pariah" dependency to growing autonomy; but this is not so much a linear progression from clientelism to interest-group pluralism as a cyclical movement responding to political stability or to crisis.

There are three phases to be noted in the transformation of the relationship between business and the authoritarian state. First, there was decay of the bureaucratic polity, during the late 1960s to early 1970s, when new entrepreneurs (like Boonchu Rojanasathien of the Bangkok Bank) foresaw greater economic opportunities under "legal-rational" constitution government than under an

---

[32] Pasuk, *Technocrats*, pp. 1–3, 6, 8–11; Medhi, "Trends," pp. 237–43; Anek, *Business Associations*, pp. 121–35. Changes in the international economy in the last three decades have been of major importance in developing Thailand's manufacturing base: communication from Kevin Hewison. See also, in regard to financial liberalization (which can "contribute significantly to sustained growth of the Thai economy"), Naris Chaiyasoot, "Industrialisation, Financial Reform, and Monetary Policy in Thailand," paper for conference on "The Making of a Fifth Tiger?: Thailand's Industrialisation and its Consequences," Australian National University, December 1992, pp. 22–23; and Suphat Suphachalasai, "Export-Led Industrialisation in Thailand," ibid., on the recent significant reductions in tariff protection: p. 10. See also Richard F. Doner and Anek Laothamatas, "The Political Economy of Structural Adjustment in Thailand," prepared for the World Bank (1992).

[33] Snoh Unakul, then Secretary-General of the NESDB as well as Secretary of the government-sponsored Joint Public/Private Sector Consultative Committee, interviewed by Anek in 1987: Anek, *Business Associations*, pp. 81–82.

arbitrary and hence unpredictable authoritarian regime which had reached the end of its tether.

The second phase, in contrast, arose as a reaction against the "turbulence" of democratic politics and student demonstrations in the mid-1970s, which depressed investor confidence both at home and abroad. Thus, business (and much of the public) approved of the 1976 military coup. In this way, "stability" was imposed on "subversion" or "anarchy." Fifteen years later, business reaction to the 1991 Suchinda coup—overthrowing the corrupt, and confrontational, Chatichai government—was rather similar.

In between such periods of turbulence, and now following the downfall of Suchinda, a third and more mature phase of business-military-political relations has appeared and continues to take shape. Business people have been increasingly aware of the domestic and international costs of old-style military intervention which upsets the new condition of "acceptable" (conservatively oriented) parliamentarism. From the business point of view, the problem no longer involves parvenu politicians, whose assertion of popular sovereignty disturbs the traditional status quo; rather, the most disturbing problems are posed by a military regime that uses brutal force against a middle-class (and working-class) public—an action now perceived as anachronistic. Nevertheless, the downside of dynamic business—as the vanguard of the new middle class—is its vested interest in the political system, both at the national, and especially at the provincial, level, as discussed below.

MONEY POLITICS

"Money politics," literally, involves trading power for wealth, and wealth for power. The first case—trading power for wealth—is characteristic of the bureaucratic polity. The second case—trading wealth for power—is typical of a "higher" level of political and economic development (though often combined with the first form). The authoritarian structure of the bureaucratic polity gives rise to situations that fit Acton's paradigm: power tends to corrupt, while "absolute power corrupts absolutely." In other words, the absence of effective checks on the state apparatus—because of the immaturity of extra-bureaucratic institutions or their lack of countervailing power—enables military or civilian authoritarian leaders to abuse their public positions for private gain. When business "clients" provide directorships or funds to political or bureaucratic "patrons" in return for protection from nationalistic—or technocratic—pressures, as well as offers of lucrative public contracts, licenses and subsidies, they are making the trade-off (power for wealth).

At a later stage of development, however, trading wealth for power is more characteristic of money politics. This is because: (1) bureaucratic authority has been eroded as a result of the rise of students, academics, other professionals, pressure groups and the media—i.e., the emergence of civil society; conversely (2), business has achieved greater autonomy as a result of some three decades of economic growth, and no longer depends on protection by powerful patrons: rather, business is acting more as an equal partner with state agencies, which cooperate for mutual advantage; finally (3), a more open, "semi-democratic," parliamentary system has evolved which not only enables political parties to have a direct input into policy decisions (often to material advantage)[34]; it also requires considerable sums of money for politicians to get elected in the first place.

Major sources of funds for politicians—at the legal level—come from business people who directly finance political parties and who may themselves become party executives and leaders: they thus have a direct stake in the political process. "Businessmen want protection [provided by] the politicians to whom they give financial support," explains the noted economist Krirkkiat Pipatseritham, rector of the University of the Thai Chamber of Commerce. That is why business people decide to enter politics: "Their main reason for doing so is that their entry will make their business much more secure." The Managing Director of the Thai Asahi Glass Company agrees: "it would be hard for a major business firm to survive if it stays away from politics." While another well-known manufacturer, Chaleao Yoowittaya, provides still another reason: "Some [businessmen] expect that their Baht 1 million donation will eventually earn them a payback of as much as Baht 100 million."[35]

Illegal inputs are the result of funding by "dark influences," especially in the provinces. Money gained by illegal gambling operations, prostitution, extortion and protection rackets, distilleries, illegal timber felling, land grabbing, and so forth can be conveniently "laundered" by way of ambitious or aspiring politicians; for the latter need ever larger sums of money to influence opinion and to buy votes. Once elected, the politician is in a position to pay back his "financier" in the normal way: by protecting illegal operations from official scrutiny and by finding new ways for both parties to make use of public projects for private gain.[36]

While the processes that propel modern businessmen into politics are relatively straightforward—political connections are needed to defend and promote their eco-

---

[34] On the "rent-seeking" activities of politically oriented business people, see Yoshiwara Kunio, *The Rise of Ersatz Capitalism in South-East Asia* (Singapore: Oxford University Press, 1988). "The capitalists who try to establish government connections for business advantage can be called rent-seekers because they are essentially seeking opportunities to become the recipients of the rent the government can confer by disposing of its resources, offering protection, or issuing authorization for certain types of activities it regulates," p. 68. For example, the government can grant a monopoly, a logging or mining concession, or a sought-after license; give protection from foreign competition, financial assistance, and a large government contract: pp. 78–79. Dictatorship has been the most fertile ground for rent-seekers, because of the lack of checks on political power, p. 86; but democracy, too, has created many rent-seekers, p. 87. See also Scott R. Christensen, "Capitalism and Democracy in Thailand," paper for Association for Asian Studies conference, Washington, D.C., April 1992, on the articulation of rent-seeking capitalism: pp. 8–9, 18–20, 33–34.

[35] "What do businessmen gain by investing in politics?": interviews in *The Nation*, March 9, 1995. Business people formed 37 percent of members of the House of Representatives in 1979, compared with some 18 percent for serving and retired government officials, and 15 percent for lawyers; in 1983 and 1986 the proportion of business people was 38 and 38.6 percent, respectively—again, more than twice the proportion of officials. In the late 1970s, businessmen formed less than 10 percent of cabinet members; but in the 1980s, between 34 and 38 percent: Likhit Dhiravegin, *Demi-Democracy: The Evolution of the Thai Political System* (Singapore: Times Academic Press, 1992), table ix, p. 222. See also Chai-Anan, "Thailand," in Diamond et al., *Politics in Developing Countries*, pp. 292–93, on the role of "political businessmen."

[36] As Chai-Anan puts it, this "mafia-type influence" emerged after the state relaxed its authoritarian control, but was still able to block the development of a bourgeois-democratic system. Provincial godfathers have become local party bosses, sponsoring electoral candidates or supporting party members. "The dilemma of Thai-style democracy is how to transform these undesirable influences into legitimate political authority": "State-Identity Creation," in Reynolds (ed.), *National Identity*, p. 80.

nomic interests—the role of "local godfathers" (*jao pho*), as Pasuk points out, is more complex. A typical *jao pho* controls a range of businesses, including retail, service and small-scale manufacture, most of which have been boosted by rising local demand. The effectiveness—and reputation—of these local businessmen as "fixers," however, is due to their combination of aggressive entrepreneurship with local political patronage, in effect creating a crucial intermediary role between the state and a wide array of local interests. Sombat's important investigation into the "influence" of *jao pho*, although differing in some respects, supports these findings.[37]

"The key to power at the local level," confirms James Ockey in a detailed study of business leaders and gangsters, is the "creation of an extensive network of ties to other influential members of society, some legitimate, some engaged in illegal activities, some in business, some in government, and some in politics." For government officials, although still powerful, are no longer able to dominate local politics on their own, as in the past.[38] To the contrary, influential *jao pho* may use their business and political connections to reward officials who cooperate in their schemes, or punish those who do not.

The preferred method, Ockey reports, is to offer officials a share of profits, either through monthly payments or through direct participation in their schemes. (Thus, one MP claimed that a province chief of police had been offered more than $10,000 a month as a pay-off for cooperation, with bonuses for "special activities.") If officials appear unwilling to cooperate in an illegal scheme, however, the *jao pho* may try to get one of the official's superiors (on the *jao pho's* payroll) to put in a timely word, or give an order, possibly backed by threats to the recalcitrant official's career.[39] (In one notorious case, in 1989, the Governor of Phichit, despite backing by the Minister of the Interior of the time, was actually forced to resign because his campaign against corruption—even though successful elsewhere—had antagonized provincial "dark influences" and notably a high ranking police officer whose source of revenue was affected.)[40]

The *jao pho's* network of connections is also suited to the ongoing electoral process. Under the *rabob hua khanaen* (system of vote-chiefs), local business interests

---

[37] Pasuk Phongpaichit, "Gift Cheques and Gin Muang: Corruption and Democracy in Thailand," research project on corruption, Political Economy Centre, Chulalongkorn University, 1992. Pasuk cites research by Andrew Turton and Sombat Chantornwong. See also · papers for conference organized by the Political Economy Centre in August 1993: "Nakturakit tekhnokhrat nakkanmuong lae naiphon: khorupchan lae anakhod khong rabob prachathipatai" [Businesspeople, technocrats, politicians, and generals: corruption and the future of the democratic system]; papers (in Thai) by Pasuk (local "godfathers"), Sungsidh (affecting public administration), Theeranat (curing corruption), Kittidet (ineffective laws), and research papers on the history of corruption (from Sarit to Chatichai), the police, and solutions. See also Sombat Chantornwong (in Thai), "The Role of Local Godfathers in Thai Economy and Politics," *Rat thun*, on *nakleng* (traditional strong and "manly" figures) and *jao pho* (godfathers, able to use their "influence," often in disregard of the law). He explains the role of the *jao pho* includes influencing officials (not to interfere in shady projects), facilitating the entry of big business into the provinces and, in general, acting as intermediary between the provincial and district authority and the villagers. *Jao pho* commonly provide benefits for village communities, thus earning their "gratitude": pp. 199, 121–27, 129–37. See also Sombat's paper for the 1993 SOAS conference, "Local Godfathers in Thai Politics."

[38] James Soren Ockey, "Business Leaders, Gangsters, and the Middle Class," PhD dissertation, Cornell University, 1992, p. 96.

[39] Ibid., p. 118.

[40] Ibid., pp. 144–50.

supply equipment, transport, and provide construction projects, as well as food and drink for the voters. The vote-chief sets up the candidate's campaign rallies, arranges parties with influential citizens, and keeps the candidate informed of weddings, religious festivals, cremations and other opportunities where he can make his presence felt. In a survey carried out by the Ministry of the Interior in 1988, for example, nearly one-third of candidates believed that such vote-buying was effective, while nearly half the voters admitted that gifts of money or material goods had affected their choice of candidate.[41] Nationwide, some 10 billion baht (about $400 million) was reportedly spent on vote-buying in the 1988 elections, and as much as 18 billion baht ($720 million) in the July 1995 elections.[42]

So effective are some of the electoral godfathers that their collective reputation has spread well beyond provincial boundaries. One such (godfather of Cholburi province following the assassination of his predecessor) played a key role in financing one of the major political parties: as a result, his mayoral celebrations were attended by the party leader, a national figure.[43] Another, whose lucrative contracts to build schools and construct roads in a central province enabled him to expand into the legal, and illegal, timber industry, "sponsored" a large number of local politicians and eventually the provincial MP. After providing large donations to this particular party (already well known for its commercial appetite), he was appointed to its central executive committee. He came to "run" some ten to twenty-five MPs, from the Center to the Northeast; and when he died (assassinated) his cremation was attended by the Minister of the Interior and four other cabinet ministers.[44] As one of the most respected of party leaders (Kukrit Pramoj) recently admitted: "Remember in politics, even if a person is *hia* [loathsome animal] you have to sleep with him if necessary. . . . You don't really have any choice. What can you do when the *hia* helps enable the government to survive?"[45]

Now, the national culmination of political openness and economic growth was the "political economy corruption" of the 1988–1991 Chatichai government, which was widely recognized to be representative of business interests. The cabinet included several members identifiable as *jao pho* or as members of Bangkok's modern

---

[41] Ibid., pp. 150–52, 159–61, 175–78. As another observer points out: "When candidates promise improved drought relief measures, new schools, donations to the local temple, and can deliver on their promise, the lives of villagers are improved. [Echoing a common assumption.] Corruption is as yet the most effective method for bringing development programs . . . to the countryside." Daniel E. King, "The Thai Parliamentary Elections of 1992," *Asian Survey*, December 1992, p. 1119.

[42] *Bangkok Post*, August 23, 1988, cited by Ockey, "Business Leaders, Gangsters," p. 179. The "vote-buying" elections in July 1995 were won by the Chart Thai party (notorious for its money politics): the Research Centre of the Thai Farmers Bank estimated that up to 17 million baht had been spent by all candidates (cited by the *Bangkok Post*).

[43] As Suchit points out, links between political faction leader and followers are based on personal ties and individual benefits. Thus, one of the major objectives of party factions is to fight for a seat in the cabinet for their leader, so that faction members, too, can have access to privileges and material advantages: Suchit, *The Military in Thai Politics*, p. 36, with examples, pp. 37, 72, 81. Prudhisan, *Nation-building*, considers that the "half-democracy" model in Thailand notably results from factional politics rather than developing "grassroots" support: pp. 114–15. Factional politics, dominated by rent-seeking activities, is the national counterpart of provincial politicking.

[44] Ockey, "Business Leaders, Gangsters," pp. 101–2, 224–25.

[45] *Bangkok Post*, August 15, 1990, quoted ibid., p. 284.

business community. Following its demise at the hands of the military, four key features of this government became clear; they are outlined in Pasuk's obituary notice:

> First, the focus was on corruption by elected politicians rather than appointed officials [as in the past]. Second, the amounts of money alleged or rumored to be involved in each case of the corruption [of 13 leading politicians found to be "unusually wealthy"] were far higher than the level seen in the past. Third, the incidents which were cited all concerned diversion of expenditure flows—particularly irregularities in the allocation of major infrastructure projects. Fourth, most of the politicians involved were clearly identifiable as elected ministers, *jao pho* or representatives of modern business.[46]

Money politics, to conclude this chilling reminder, arises from an "excess" of supply (ambitious politicians, with access to public funds) and demand (ambitious entrepreneurs on the make). Indeed, the combination of capitalism, spurred on by the profit motive, and democracy (or democratization), which generates ever-growing requirements to fund electoral competition, results in "political economy corruption," also known as the "unacceptable face of capitalism." In principle, such a combination should not have occurred: for democracy—"the will of the people"—has exclusive claims in theory to regulate society. In practice, however, no politician in a modernizing society can afford to ignore the interests of business. To maintain economic "confidence" and international "competitiveness," even politicians of integrity have to compromise between the interests of the public (as pledged electorally) and the imperatives of the economy. And if politicians are not persons of integrity then collusion (with business) easily turns into corruption.[47]

Money politics—that is to say, corruption—is therefore born of the incongruity— the "misfitting"— between the claims of democracy (popular sovereignty) and the exigencies of capitalism (the economic basis of state power). Corruption is not merely a matter of economic definition, however, for in the growth of capitalism one source of profit is as valid as any other. Rather, corruption is *normatively* defined. It is in these terms that corruption is seen as the "abuse" of public position for private gain—derogating from the common good. This is the significance of the king's remarkable address in July 1995—following the election victory of the Chart Thai leader, Banharn Silpa-Archa, and his cabinet appointments—when he emphasized the utmost need for government to act with ability, honesty, justice, and moral strength if the country, the people, and the democratic system were to prosper and progress. The speech demonstrates the depth of concern of such a highly respected figure about the debased standards of public life.[48]

Thus, in spite of the prevalence of corruption in modernizing (as well as in "advanced") countries, such normative standards remain important, and particularly in the case of civil society (discussed in the next chapter). Consider the absence of public outrage at the overthrow of the Chatichai government, which testified to the

---

[46] Pasuk, "Gift Cheques," pp. 30–31.

[47] For a more general discussion, with case studies, see the author's *Corruption, Capitalism, and Democracy*, to be published by Routledge, London.

[48] The king also emphasized the need for "legitimacy," using the English word. See text in *Matichon Sudsapda*, August 22, 1995.

moral alienation of ordinary citizens in regard to cabinet ministers possessing "unusual wealth." Conversely, the outrage of that same public some fifteen months later demonstrated their moral refusal to grant legitimacy to an unelected military prime minister, who had reneged on his promise not to take power.

Money politics reveals a further contradiction (also discussed in the next chapter) between the *urban* concentration of military and business power and *rural* society, where a majority of people still live, but whose economic contribution is in substantial decline. Rural society furnishes the soldiers—for the military leaders to use against civil society. It provides staple crops for export, which for a long time were taxed to subsidize the (wealthier) urban population. It is discriminated against by Bangkok in the provision of government services. And yet despite all this, it sells its votes to maintain the most conservative, pro-military, or commercialized political parties in power—or with a share of power—enabling them to perpetuate an unfair distribution of wealth and power.[49] The *interaction* of wealth and power is summarized below.

THE RANGE OF BUSINESS-POLITICAL RELATIONS

(1) The general climate of economic growth has altered the balance between power and wealth in Thailand. More than thirty years of expansion have radically transformed Thailand, and this transformation has reached from the capital to the countryside. Booming real estate, inauguration of a stock exchange, spread of financial services and industrialization, formation of a middle class (and beginnings of a working class), increasing migration from the provinces, urban development and slums, agribusiness, contract farming, mechanization of agriculture, commercialization and consumerism: these are striking indications of change, affecting economic outlook and occupational careers, political institutions (including access to funds, patronage distribution of largesse) and social values. Wealth is esteemed more highly than bureaucratic status, reversing the old order. The drift of talented individuals away from the poorly paid civil service to the private sector provides evidence of this reversal. So does the wide, popular acceptance of the maxim that Thailand must maintain business—and international—"confidence." As a consequence, even the military has been forced to recognize the disruptive impact on society—and especially the economy—of its customary weapon, the coup.

(2) Technocrats have played a major role in facilitating economic growth, in effect, linking the bureaucracy and parliamentary government with the business sector. Since the days of Sarit, technocrats have rationalized the bureaucratic structure of decision making, favoring efficiency, transparency, and regularity. Technocratic decisions in the 1980s, under successive Prem governments, contributed largely to the resolution of economic crises (even at the expense of military interests). The technocrats confirmed over the years Thailand's reputation for "responsible" fiscal and monetary policies; and they effectively promoted the country's export orientation. Have they worked for democracy as well? This is a difficult question to answer. As a body, technocrats strive for efficient government, not necessarily demo-

---

[49] Thailand's seventh national economic and social development plan (1992–96) reports that disparities in income distribution have "increased to an alarming level": the income of the top 20 percent has grown from 49.3 percent of the total in 1975/76 to 54.9 percent in 1987/88; that of the lowest 20 percent has fallen from 6.1 percent to only 4.5 percent. Agricultural workers, for example, receive only about half the national average income. NESDB, 7th plan, p. 2.

cratic government. Their preference, to put it in different terms, is for order rather than freedom or justice.

(3) The institutionalization of economic-political linkages was a significant feature of the 1980s. Joint consultative committees of leading business associations (finance, industry, and commerce) and bureaucratic departments and government ministries functioned under the aegis of the technocrats. By the end of the 1980s, however, the influence both of technocrats and joint committees declined, as politicians in the Chatichai government made their own economic decisions. This laissez-faire attitude has persisted with the revival of parliamentary government from 1992.

(4) Direct political participation by individual businessmen has been evident since the first democratic period in the 1970s. Businessmen have financed political parties and, when elected as deputies, have competed for the post of cabinet minister—especially those in control of departments deciding on profitable public contracts. Indeed, by the 1980s metropolitan and especially provincial businessmen had displaced serving and retired officials as the largest category in the elected house of representatives.

(5) The conjunction of business interest in politics with the preponderance of rural voters has been significant. The latter, seeking a "return" from the electoral system (to make up for their disadvantaged economic situation), participate in large-scale vote-buying organized by local "fixers," on the one hand, and receive patronage "paybacks" from successful politicians, channeling public resources to their constituents, on the other. "Money politics," whatever its economic benefits to particular clients, impedes the attainment of an independent and impartial democracy.

(6) The distortions of "development" and "democracy in the Thai style." It is the distributional, rather than the productive, aspect of the economic system that is most at fault. Nevertheless, for the distributional shortcomings the political system must also bear responsibility. The political system, as Christensen points out, has performed well for specific interest groups and voters, but it has not provided policies that effectively address the collective needs of a rapidly industrializing society. This style of government is the result of "Bangkok-based development," which has had the following consequences:

> Over the past three decades, adjustments to the institutions of national decision-making have strengthened the central government's control over the provinces and boosted the role of urban industrialists in the policy-making process. While gradually improving the state's policy management capacities, these adjustments have had pernicious distributional consequences as well. They have centered most of the industrial growth in and around Bangkok; served the political interests of the capital's bureaucratic elite; and assigned urban industrialists a privileged status in policy making.[50]

The intimate relationship between Bangkok-based development and the emerging "hegemony" of the middle class is analyzed in the following chapter.

---

[50] Scott R. Christensen, *Democracy without Equity?: The Institutions and Political Consequences of Bangkok-based Development* (Bangkok: Thailand Development Research Institute: 1993 Year-End Conference), pp. iii–iv; also 2–3, 12–16.

3

THE MIDDLE CLASS AND CIVIL SOCIETY

MIDDLE CLASS AND ALTERNATIVES

The middle class is generally perceived to be a heterogeneous grouping, comprising: civil servants, and academics; salaried employees of the majority of modern business; small businesspersons and shopkeepers; and independent professionals. Each of these groups, as a direct or indirect result of economic development, has expanded enormously over the years.[1]

In size, the urban middle class is, of course, only a small part of the total (largely rural) population. But such numbers are static indicators. More significant is the dynamic relationship between the middle class, the economic system, state power, and civil society.

Dominating the middle class, as the driving force of the modern economy, is its financial, industrial and commercial elite. "Big business," or the "bourgeoisie," establishes the parameters for subordinate groups in society, both by creating or underpinning their economic existence and by asserting and defining a materialistic way of life that is widely aspired to by others in society. Pragmatism, materialism, individualism: these can be considered the core values of the middle class.

The "achievement" outlook of the middle class and its elite is now prevalent in society, because of the disappearance or erosion of alternatives, whether on the tra-

---

[1] Scott R. Christensen and Ammar Siamwalla, *Beyond Patronage: Tasks for the Thai State* (Bangkok: Thailand Development Research Institute, 1993 Year-End Conference), p. 26, referring to "middle classes." In my view, however, there are unifying (as well as discordant) interests and values; accordingly, I prefer "middle class." Voravidh Charoenlert also points to the homogeneous character of the Thai middle class in terms of income and work security: "The Middle Class and May 1992" (in Thai), in Sungsidh Piriyarangsan and Pasuk Phongpaichit (eds.), *Chonchun klang bonkrasae prachathipatai thai* [the middle class and Thai democratization] (Bangkok: Political Economy Centre, Chulalongkorn University, 1993), p. 133. In numbers, the Thai middle class has doubled since 1970 and now comprises about one-fifth of the employed population; this is not far short of the urban working population (some 22 percent in 1989): Report of Labor Force Survey, National Statistical Office, cited by Pasuk Phongpaichit and Chris Baker, "Jao Sua, Jao Poh, Jao Tii: Lords of Thailand's Transition," paper for 5th International Conference on Thai Studies, London, SOAS, July 1993. More generally on the middle class, see Richard Robison and David S. G. Goodman (eds.) *The New Rich in Asia* (London: Routledge, 1996). Note the editors' distinction between capital-owning bourgeoisie and professional middle classes, the latter ranging from "highly paid professionals and managers to the village school teacher and postal clerk." p. 5; critical factors in the formation of the middle class are living standards, education, legal framework, and access to information. p. 11. On Thailand, see Kevin Hewison's chapter in *The New Rich in Asia*, pp. 141-45, 154-56.

ditional right or the radical left. According to the Gramscian theory of "hegemony" (leadership, not by force, but by consent) a fundamental class imposes its own vision of what society stands for—an outlook that is accepted, consciously or otherwise, by the majority.

Middle class hegemony is central to the logic of economic development; it is the wave of the future. Even if the middle class does not yet dominate the power structure—there is still "dislocation" as well as overlap between economic and political structures—its materialist values permeate both the military and the civilian bureaucracy. Indeed, the once-dominant military is more and more on the defensive: as a result of the collapse of the Communist Party of Thailand followed by Vietnam's economic conversion to capitalism, "national security" no longer provides a convincing legitimation of military rule.

The civilian bureaucrats, too, are fighting a rearguard action—but more effectively against the encroachments of elected politicians than of business. Throughout Thailand, the authority of bureaucratic officials is giving way to the wealth and influence of provincial and metropolitan entrepreneurs. The technocrats, to be sure, remain influential players, but their role in pressing for greater transparency, efficiency, and rationality in the administration and in the economy is precisely in accordance with the interests of modern business, and of the professional middle class.

The middle class is achieving its hegemony, positively, in symbiosis with economic development, and negatively, by default of other once-powerful or influential alternatives. It is important to consider this "default" in more detail—that is, the absence of presumed alternatives offered by the military, the civil service, rural society and, to the left, the forming urban working class.

First of all, the military has long been "subverted" by material values. "Trading generals" were ubiquitous in the days of Sarit, Thanom, and Prapart. As for the economic interests of present-day faction leaders, they have simply become more modernized—taking the shape of military-owned construction firms and arms procurement deals. The Class 5 group took a special interest in construction projects and arms trading, for example. Military officers still play a role in provincial business, especially in projects involving land. And state authorities, often headed by prominent military figures, provide "massive patronage in the form of contracts for construction and supply—buying aircraft, installing telephone lines, launching satellites."[2] As for the military's long-expected transformation into an increasingly "professional" organization—a transformation whose prospects the 1992 crisis has improved—such professionalism, including non-involvement in politics, would certainly bring the military more into line with middle-class practices, as in Japan and the West.

Admittedly, even the increasingly prominent role of business, at home and abroad, does not in itself rule out further coup attempts. But these will more and more be seen, both in Thailand and especially internationally, as arbitrary, anachronistic, and disruptive, perhaps acceptable in the short term, but not as an enduring feature of a modernizing society. Indeed, business people are replacing the military as the most influential factor in Thai politics, according to academics interviewed by

---

[2] Pasuk Phongpaichit and Chris Baker, *Thailand: Economy and Politics* (Kuala Lumpur: Oxford University Press, 1995), chapter on "The Military and Democracy."

The Nation (March 9, 1995). "Nowadays, political influence is tantamount to business influence," as Somchai Pakapaswiwat from Thammasat University points out.

Like the military, although to a lesser degree, the administrative civil service retains considerable negative power, for example over parliamentary legislation, and in regulating business activities. But as an institution it is losing out to the private sector in terms of function, employment, and career prospects.

As two perceptive researchers point out:

Thailand is experiencing a rapid shift from an administrative-centered to an interest-centered government, whereby individuals and groups from various quarters of society have penetrated the State and are increasingly shaping the goods and services it supplies. . . .

Many of the services the State now needs to provide, however, particularly in sectoral policy areas are heavily knowledge-intensive and require administrative and technological sophistication. But the State has been designed institutionally to supply public services and patronage in a top-down fashion at the hest of its officials, and it is increasingly unable to procure coherent, effective policies for a more complex and demanding society. As industrialization and massive urbanization proceed, the old institutions and ways of conducting policy will no longer do if the country is to remain competitive globally while also distributing the gains of growth more equitably among all sectors of the population.[3]

The problem is more than a matter of functional incapacity. For the authors refer to "an underskilled, underpaid, and increasingly demoralized civil service." Thus, there has been a "stunning decline" in incomes among civil service employees. The income of a permanent secretary stands at about 15 percent of the value of the equivalent salary in 1909. Admittedly, for senior civil servants, "their access to state enterprise boards, national policy committees, and connections with private sector clientele provide sources of income that help to compensate for their trifle [trifling] salaries."[4] The conclusion drawn by a World Bank survey is worth noting: while "the civil service has become a meritocratic institution, senior officials remain vulnerable to the influence of business interests and patronage remains part of the system."[5]

Unlike the elitism of bureaucratic institutions—now increasingly infiltrated by middle-class values—the "alternative" visions of the left are mass-based. As such, they reflect not only the situation of the rural majority, but also the expectation of a more modern (even dominant) role to be played by the urban "proletariat." In both cases, however, such ideologically driven alternatives have proved deceptive.

Marxism assumes that revolutionary movements erupt where there is greater economic development and social dislocation, and yet central Thailand, where tenancy and landlessness are prevalent, has shown few signs of resistance, let alone revolt. To the contrary, the Communist Party of Thailand was most effective (for a time) in remote or marginal areas of the country. Moreover, the CPT's vision of an

---

[3] Christensen and Ammar, *Beyond Patronage*, p. 2; see also pp. 3, 5, 7, 8, 12, 20–24.

[4] Ibid., pp. 14, 17–18. Apart from such specific inducements, there are few incentives for a qualified professional to make the civil service a lifetime vocation: p. 18.

[5] Scott Christensen, David Dollar, Ammar Siamwalla, and Pakorn Vichyanond, *Thailand: The Institutional and Political Underpinnings of Growth* (Washington, D.C.: World Bank, 1993), p. x; also p. 20.

alternative society has been discredited by the failure of communist practices (and not least the Maoist variants) worldwide.

Rather, Thailand's rural population has responded to economic change in two ways: either by spontaneous resistance to particular projects (huge dams, eucalyptus plantations, forest clearances, etc.)—a resistance that is often ecologically (middle class) inspired; or by accommodation to the system (contract farming, crop diversification, use of credit, mechanization, etc.). It is precisely the mid-level farmers (estimated to be about 50 to 70 percent of cultivators) whose role is especially important in improving production, establishing markets, and exploiting new technologies. It is the poor and landless (20 to 30 percent) who are the losers.[6]

Moreover, the political response of the people of the countryside takes the form, as noted, of selling votes to politicians in return for expected material benefits from the successful candidates.

Such a pragmatic role, born of inability to change the system, also characterizes the formation of an urban working class. The latter still bears the imprint of its rural origins and, indeed, of the "informal economy" to which many from the countryside gravitate in the towns and cities. Even in the modern sector, job insecurity, poor pay, and a precarious lifestyle prevail. Workers, as a result, are preoccupied directly with the improvement of their material conditions.

Such organizations as do exist—the trade unions in the public and private sectors—tend to be weak, divided by factional struggles, and often bought or manipulated by leading politicians or bureaucrats as part of a wider patronage network. Actively reformist unions (radicals have usually been suppressed) do, however, strive to get a better bargain for their members within the system.

Thus, in the absence of convincing alternatives, either from the right or the left, the middle class gains by default. Such an interpretation is not incompatible with Niddhi's very critical analysis of the Thai middle class. He assumes that it has lost its bourgeois world outlook—in favor of democracy, equality, freedom, and the rule of law—and come to rely instead on wealth and power, divorced from any "philosophical foundation" on which to sustain its resources and its power.[7] But, in my view, the middle class is more differentiated in its practice and its outlook. Part of it—perhaps the leading part—is materialistic and power-driven; but another part, inspired by civil society, is reform-minded and idealistic. As another analyst emphasizes, the middle class is homogeneous in its occupational character (income and security); but under certain conditions some members can become radicals, supporting the left, and others liberals, advocating democracy.[8]

---

[6] Pasuk Phongpaichit, "Farmers, the State, and Capitalists" (in Thai), in Pasuk and Sungsidh Piriyarangsan (eds.), *Phonlawat thai: Mummong jak sethsat kanmuang* [Thai Dynamics: a political economy view] (Bangkok: Political Economy Centre, Chulalongkorn University, 1991), pp. 54–63.

[7] Niddhi Aewsriwong, "Culture of the Thai Middle Class" (in Thai), in Sungsidh and Pasuk (eds.), *Chonchun klang*, pp. 60-65.

[8] Voravidh, "The Middle Class" (in Thai), in Sungsidh and Pasuk, *Chonchun klang*, pp. 133–35; on the political economy definition of the middle class, pp. 126–27. In Thanet Apornsuwan's view, capitalist development has had a major impact on Thai society and civil society (the rule of law), but cannot create a stable bourgeois democracy, because of the resistance of bureaucratic leaders seeking to retain power in the old way [reflecting the impact of the 1991 coup]: Thanet, "State and Thai Politics in the 1990s" (in Thai), in Pasuk Phongpaichit and Sungsidh Piriyarangsan (eds.), *Rat thun jaopho thongthin kab sangkhom thai* [The state,

Pragmatism, materialism, individualism: these, at last, are the core values of the middle class, for they are the social product of economic development, which sweeps aside bureaucratic honor and prestige (*barami*), on the one hand, and rural "community culture" and urban working-class "proletarianism," on the other.

For in Thailand there is no homogeneous "social block" of workers, with a common identity. Instead, the working class (and, in its own way, the peasantry) has been disaggregated by technological innovation, precarious work conditions, mobility of labor, and unemployment. In occupational terms, the middle class, too, has become increasingly differentiated as a result of the rise in service occupations, the dominance of financial institutions, the widening scope of industrial joint ventures, and integration into the world market. On the other hand, formerly powerful political ideologies (communism, fascism) influencing the different classes have virtually disappeared, giving way to a consumerist middle-class culture.

Undoubtedly, the vast expansion of education (required for effective economic development) has directly contributed to the new status of the middle class. While three-quarters of those with secondary education and above worked for the government in 1970, in the next two decades nearly two million more received a similar education, and over 60 percent of the expansion went into the private sector.[9]

Culturally, television has also played its role. "The night-time television drama became a nationally shared cultural experience. The most popular type were family dramas which dealt with social changes and issues relevant to the audience. Many dramas dealt with the struggle of the new middle class to achieve worldly success while retaining their souls. . . ."[10]

The struggle between self-interest and idealism for the "soul" of the middle class reflects the perennial dilemma of the need for order competing against the desire for freedom and justice. Evidently, the economic interests of the middle class require stable conditions—for the sake of investment, production, and long-term returns. This requirement of stability may well be provided by authoritarian regimes: such as Soeharto's regime in Indonesia or the former bureaucratic polity in Thailand. But an erratic, violence-prone military—as demonstrated under present conditions in Thailand—no longer provides such a guarantee. Recognizing this development, industrialists, financiers, and traders opt for "democratization"—that is, they turn to the conservative elements of civil society, who dominate parliamentary and professional institutions instead of relying on the military to enforce stability.

But even middle class "order" does not lack a component of "freedom" and "justice." Political freedom (to form parties, to campaign for elections) has its economic counterpart in "free enterprise" and consumer choice. As for justice, an established and impartial legal system is a precondition both for economic expansion and for political expression. Order and justice are therefore not mutually exclusive—even if they are located at opposite ends of the scale.

Conversely, certain progressive elements of the middle class, in sympathy with advocates from the wider ambit of civil society (including rural organizers and trade union leaders), are more concerned with justice than order, because they perceive a

capitalists, local mafia, and Thai society] (Bangkok: Political Economy Centre, Chulalongkorn University, 1992), p. 217.

[9] Pasuk and Baker, "Towards Civil Society," *Thailand: Economy and Politics.*

[10] Ibid.

need to redress the balance of an unequal society; but they also must operate within a framework of orderly expectations.

Thai development can therefore be interpreted as a "field of force" in which previously autonomous elements—from mid-level peasants to authoritarian bureaucrats—are losing their separate identities as they succumb to the economic attraction (and the values) of the middle class. But partly as a result of its absorption or attraction of other social strata, this middle class is far from homogeneous—as the tension between order and justice shows.

It is in this dual context of middle class ascendancy, on the one hand, with differing visions of society, on the other, that I propose to analyze the varying elements of civil society. To repeat: there are no longer convincing radical or traditional *alternatives* to the core values of the middle class (pragmatism, materialism, individualism); but, *within* the middle class, there exist "preferential" values (ranging from order to justice) that may cooperate or conflict with the fundamentally pragmatic, materialistic values. The core values are necessary to the existence of the middle class. But they also permit the expression of preferential (individual) values, so long as these do not directly threaten what is fundamental. (Idealists, it should be recalled, usually come from comfortable backgrounds. But this is not to deny the valuable contribution of idealism!) For it is precisely the concern of those who *prefer* freedom and justice (the democratic values), and who assert normative standards as against the "conservative" reality, which encourages prospects for a more equitable development.

In this chapter, the task is to analyze in more detail the interest and values of the various social groupings discussed above, in the context of the ascendant middle class. (The military, as a regressive force, was considered in the previous chapter.) I associate each category or class with a particular "solution" for society and then try to assess—in concrete terms—the extent to which each has become a motivating force for social change, for renewal. (Note that because of constraints on time, opportunity, and knowledge I merely sketch, and certainly do not "establish," the theoretical solution for each category and its realization, or lack of realization.) These, then, are hypotheses that are presented for confirmation, amendment, or refutation—for debate, in other words—that may contribute to a fuller explanation.

My range of hypotheses starts with the Maoist strategy of "countryside encircling towns," which animated the Communist Party of Thailand for many years. There follows a discussion of "everyday" forms of peasant resistance, on the one hand, and proletarian/trade union struggle, on the other. Turning to the middle class, the "Modernization theory" inspiring middle-class professionals is compared with the logic undergirding "traditional" patron-client relations; such an analysis involves "modernization" and bureaucratic "tradition" as both organizing principles and practices. Similarly, corporatist structures suited to modern business and technocracy are compared with the more dynamic, and disturbing, "circulation of the elites," and with Marxist critiques of "bourgeois democracy." I end with the normative values of civil society, as expressed chiefly by non-governmental organizations: religious affirmations, the struggle for human rights, participatory democracy, eradication of poverty, rural self-reliance, and defense of the environment.

In each case, evidently, there is division—in class struggle as in the struggle for human rights, and in other "NGO" issues—between powerful abusers and "local" defenders. Division is equally explicit in situations where corporate managers exert controls over the non-privileged workforce, just as it exists in the superior/subordinate relationship between patron and client. Division is implicit even in the modernization model of capitalist democracy, where economic interests must prevail if the system is to survive. Nevertheless, out of division comes the possibility for renewal.

RURAL STRUGGLE: COUNTRYSIDE SURROUNDS CITIES

The revolutionary movement led by the Communist Party of Thailand flourished in the 1960s and 1970s, especially in the remoter areas of the Northeast and among ethnic minorities in the North and South. But the CPT collapsed in the early 1980s, and is now no longer an alternative either to authoritarian or democratizing regimes. Why, when conditions seemed "ripe" for a Maoist-type rural revolution, did the CPT fall apart?

In the Northeast, as one specialist observed at the time, "the basic causes of insurgency revolve primarily around poor economic and social conditions—i.e., low wages, land alienation, high land rentals, administrative inefficiency and corruption, and inadequate educational services."[11] Poor and arid soils are a basic problem (rather than tenancy) in this region, where the per capita income is only half the national average and where, at the time, nearly three-quarters of rural families lived below the poverty line.

More critical than the economic situation, however, was the way in which villagers related to the political and administrative system. "In their personal contacts with government officials—civilian, police and military—the villagers frequently were treated badly, with disdain, exploitation, and discourtesy. Corruption was rampant at all levels of government, and any villagers exposed to it could only reach the conclusion that each official was interested primarily in lining his own pockets, at the expense of his own countrymen and of the country itself." On their own, villagers could do little about their feeling of being maltreated:

> All this changed in a profound way, however, when the CPT's village organizer arrived on the scene. Working with the unique set of grievances in that individual village, the village organizer offered the villagers a sense of unity and organizational focus for acting upon their anger and sense of injustice. "Join with me," the cadre says, "and we will replace this corrupt, unfair government with one of our own, from the people themselves."[12]

While economic and social conditions favored the revolutionary movement in "peripheral" areas, for a long time a national focus was lacking. What dramatically changed this situation was the influx of student radicals, fleeing to the jungle after the bloody 1976 military coup. At last the Maoist formula of national cause (expressed by amalgamation with urban radicals) and social conditions (in the rural areas) seemed to have been realized. Yet at the precise time when the flood tide of communism crested, the revolutionary movement began to regress. The students'

[11] Robert F. Zimmerman, "Insurgency in Thailand," *Problems of Communism*, May–June 1976, quoted in John L. S. Girling, *Thailand: Society and Politics* (Ithaca, New York: Cornell University Press, 1981), pp. 258–59.

[12] David Morell and Chaianan Samudavanija, *Political Conflict in Thailand: Reform, Reaction, Revolution* (Cambridge, Mass.: Oelgeschlager, Gunn, and Hain, 1981), pp. 90–91; see also pp. 121, 152–53, and the informative chapter, "Changing Revolutionary Capabilities," pp. 285–308.

own contribution to revolution highlighted basic contradictions within the party itself.

A major contradiction was the party's dogmatic belief that Thailand was only at the "semi-feudal, semi-colonial" stage of development, as in China in the 1920s and 1930s, when Mao had formulated his doctrine of "people's war." The student radicals argued, to the contrary, that Thailand was already being transformed by capitalism: this was something that the students were well aware of in their everyday lives, even if the party leaders—isolated in their rural strongholds—were not. Moreover, the ethnic Chinese origins of the veteran party leaders predisposed them to the Maoist strategy, while the students, on the other hand, sought to develop a more independent, national line. Finally, the doctrinaire party members refused to consider the students as equal partners, rejecting any notion of theoretical compromise or synthesis of urban-rural viewpoints.[13]

The conjuncture of three events transformed the uneasy standoff between party and students into outright alienation, leading to the party's virtual disintegration. First, the Kringsak government granted amnesty to student rebels in the late 1970s. Second, a dispute arose between the two countries where communism had triumphed—China and Vietnam—culminating in war (unthinkable for believers in communist solidarity); the consequence was the Vietnamese decision to close Indochinese supply routes and sanctuaries to the pro-China CPT. Finally, a matter that profoundly shocked Thai communists and radicals alike: Beijing initiated conciliatory moves, for reasons of global Realpolitik, toward rapprochement with the Thai government and class enemy of the CPT. In conclusion, the radicals drifted back to the cities, under the government's amnesty policy, while the party, cut off from its "rear base," disheartened by ideological splits, and outmatched by government forces, came to abandon the unequal struggle.

PEASANTS: EVERYDAY FORMS OF RESISTANCE

Revolutionary activity by the peasantry is exceptional; it is still more exceptional for it to succeed. James Scott, in his pioneering study, rightly points out that subordinate classes are rarely afforded the luxury of large-scale, organized political activity. The social structure of the peasantry—scattered, unorganized, defensive—is better suited to "everyday" forms of resistance: "the prosaic but constant struggle between the peasantry and those who seek to extract labor, food, taxes, rents, and interest from them." Such forms of struggle often stop well short of outright collective defiance of the economic or political system. Instead, they are the "weapons of the weak"—foot-dragging, dissimulation, desertion, pilfering, feigned ignorance, slander, arson, sabotage, and so on.[14]

---

[13] Note the illuminating comments by student leaders interviewed by Yuangrat Wedel, *The Thai Radicals and the Communist Party* (Singapore: Maruzen Asia and Institute of Southeast Asian Studies, 1983). The CPT regarded the radicals as "urbanized intellectuals"—the very antithesis of the peasants who should bear the revolution. "They (CPT) tried to get us to eliminate ourselves. They stressed sacrifice, unthinking labour, patience and unquestioning obedience." p. 16. It was not so much the ethnic Chinese origins of CPT leaders that upset the students as their complete allegiance to Chinese ideas and attitudes, which was unacceptable to students motivated by the need for a Thai revolution. p. 24. Students argued for the importance of the emerging capitalist class in Thailand, while the CPT hardly acknowledged its existence. pp. 32–33, 38–39, 55–56.

[14] James C. Scott, *Weapons of the Weak: Everyday Forms of Peasant Resistance* (New Haven, Conn.: Yale University Press, 1985), Preface. This is a rich and fascinating work, with generalizations

These forms of struggle are not focused solely on issues concerning work, property rights, grain and cash, but also on the "appropriation of symbols": how to understand the past, to identify causes, to assess blame; in other words, how to give a particular meaning to local history. This "war of symbols" reflects the wider struggle of elites to impose their own image of a just social order, not simply as a way to influence the behavior of non-elites, but their consciousness as well. It also reflects the struggle of ordinary people to resist that imposed image and to insist on an alternative. Thus, the views of the poor as to what counts for "decent" conduct—by selective appeals to customary practices—are all bent towards a normative outlook that serves their material and symbolic interests.

The capitalist transformation of the countryside, however, not only undermines the material interests of the poorer peasants, it also affects the behavior of the well-to-do. Their change to a market orientation (away from the traditional belief in the social obligations of propertied individuals) implies a decision to change from the exercise of moral authority to the exercise of economic authority: relying on law, property rights, coercion and political patronage.[15]

It is this "revolutionary" shift away from customary values—which oblige the rich to help the poor in times of need—toward an acceptance of the impersonal operation of market forces that the poor try to resist, not by open confrontation, which is too risky, but by "everyday" forms of protest. For example, in Thailand, many poor farmers are critical, but fear to "speak up." It is only when poor farmers hold their own meetings without the presence of richer farmers and village officials that they "dare to show their feelings."[16]

While Scott initially claims that such individual acts of evasion and dissimulation, when "multiplied many thousand-fold," may effectively subvert state policies—or at least close off some options—his conclusion is pessimistic. In the context of the revolutionary changes brought about by capitalism, he argues, poorer peasants look to the values that have proved effective in the past to defend themselves in the future. Their goals of resistance are as modest as their values: to gain work, land, and income—not to aspire to such historical abstractions as socialism, let alone Marxism-Leninism. Their means are prudent and realistic: when flight is available (such as migration to the cities) it is taken; when confrontation with state or capitalist power seems futile, it is avoided. Generalizing from such negative examples of "resistance," Scott admits to "a certain pessimism" about the prospects that would respect even the "small decencies" that are at the core of peasant or working-class consciousness.[17]

This conclusion would seem to be borne out by conditions in Thailand. Peasant revolution spread—for a time—in the poorest and economically least developed regions. But where capitalism had its greatest impact, and social polarization would therefore seem to be most acute—between better-off farmers and landless laborers, for example, in the Central Plain—the political consequences, along Marxist lines,

drawn worldwide, from the past to the present, although the main case study is from Malaysia.

[15] Ibid., pp. 38–39, 310–12.

[16] Andrew Turton, "Limits of Ideological Domination and the Formation of Social Consciousness," in A. Turton and S. Tanabe (eds.), *History and Peasant Consciousness in Southeast Asia* (Osaka: National Museum of Ethnology, 1984).

[17] Scott, *Weapons of the Weak*, pp. xvii, 35–36, 348–50.

have not developed. Neither farmers nor laborers, in Chai-Anan's view, have developed from a class in itself into a "class for itself."[18] (See also the more extensive discussion of rural development—from the standpoint of NGOs—in the last section of this chapter.)

WORKING CLASS

Rather than thinking of socialism "in the completely logical consistent sense," according to George Orwell, the ordinary worker adopts a more immediate, pragmatic attitude: for the worker, "socialism does not mean much more than better wages and shorter hours and nobody bossing you about." (It is only among middle-class intellectuals that orthodoxy prevails.)[19] This is the "trade union consciousness"—and not revolutionary militancy—that Lenin derided before 1917.

In Thailand, too, "trade unionism" seems more appropriate to economic conditions and to working-class consciousness. The Thai working class is not a monolithic entity, but is divided in at least three ways: between workers in the organized sector and in the informal economy; between female and male workers; and between workers in the public and in the private sector. Each type either has different experiences and different interests to defend, or has different ways of defending the same interests.

Of some five million people in the urban labor force (in 1988), just over half were in the informal sector. Some 52 percent in the informal economy were female workers—and as much as 60 percent in the organized sector. Women workers, reputedly cheap and docile, are well represented in the textile and garment industry.[20] The plight of women workers was horribly demonstrated in the 1993 fire at the Kader Industrial toy factory in Bangkok—a disaster that caused the highest number of deaths in such circumstances in world history.

Workers in the informal sector are both less likely to be educated and less likely to earn a substantial salary. As many as three-quarters of all workers in the informal sector have only elementary education, compared with less than one-third in the organized economy.[21] The importance of education in obtaining a better income has been amply demonstrated. In agriculture and mining, for example, workers with only elementary education received (in 1984) an average of some 450–500 baht a month, which was less than half the income earned by those graduating from secondary school. As for manufacturing and services, workers with elementary education received between 1,300 and 1,700 baht a month; while those at secondary school level earned between 2,300 and 2,600 baht, and university graduates some 6,800 baht on average. Workers in electronics and car servicing earned the highest average manual wage (around 11,000 baht); construction workers, with poor living

---

[18] Chai-Anan Samudavanija, "Thailand: A Stable Semi-Democracy," in Larry Diamond, Juan J. Linz, and Seymour Martin Lipset (eds.), *Politics in Developing Countries: Comparing Experiences with Democracy* (Boulder, Colo.: Lynne Rienner, 1990), p. 302.

[19] Orwell, *The Road to Wigan Pier* (1939), quoted by Scott, *Weapons of the Weak*, p. 349.

[20] Pasuk Phongpaichit, "The Urban Informal Sector," in Pasuk and Shigeru Itoga (eds.), *The Informal Sector in Thai Informal Development* (Tokyo: Institute of the Developing Economies, 1991), pp. 19, 28–29. See also Sungsidh Piriyarangsan, "Industrial development and Labor relations" (in Thai), in Pasuk and Sungsidh (eds.), *Rat thun,* on the division between formal and informal workers, table p. 296, wage conditions, pp. 303–8, and women workers, especially tables, pp. 314–15, 317.

[21] Pasuk, "Urban Informal Sector," p. 19.

conditions (and low education), earned the least. Finally, unskilled females and teenagers (many of them, like construction workers, migrants from rural areas) usually earned less than the minimum wage.[22]

Typically, in the informal sector, women workers and teenagers live with the shopowner, who subcontracts textile and ready-made garments for retailers and exporters. Their work hours are not fixed, but are generally from eight o'clock in the morning to midnight, with two meals provided and Sunday off. Workers may earn from 6 to 7 baht for a short-sleeve shirt, while the shopowner gets up to 16 baht for each item from the wholesale merchant (who sells the shirt at 120–130 baht). Shopowners and workers work together, like a big family, with time to talk and joke and listen to country music. Yet many of the young workers come unwillingly (sent by their parents) and lack motivation and seriousness. The owner, in paternalistic style, then has to demonstrate authority, perhaps by keeping part of the wage in reserve or sending it directly to the parents.[23] Such subcontracting practices in the informal sector keeps the cost of production low and helps increase exports (textiles and garments amounted to 37 percent of total exports in 1987).[24]

Union organization does not exist under such conditions. Yet, even in the "organized" sector, union members form only a small proportion of all workers: some 300,000 in 1990 out of an urban workforce of nearly five million. More than half of union members belong to public sector enterprises and services. These unions were banned by the military "peace-keeping" authority following the February 1991 coup. State sector unions have since been authorized by the Chuan government, but the ban on strikes remains. Unions in any case have long been subject to control or manipulation by powerful personalities.[25]

Except for the brief period between 1973 and 1976, when strikes were almost a daily occurrence, "the workforce is no longer militant, with only an estimated 5 percent represented by unions":

> Cheap labor, a docile workforce, no strikers and generally favorable work practices, along with readily available natural resources, are conditions very much sought after by international business and the major foreign powers. A quick perusal of some economic facts confirms that Thailand scores high in all the areas mentioned.[26]

---

[22] Kitti Limskul, "Source of Economic Growth Owing to Education and Labour Quality," in Chira Hongladarom and Shigeru Itoga (eds.), *Human Resources Development Strategy in Thailand* (Tokyo: Institute of Developing Economies, 1991), pp. 25, 56–57, 68, 87. In contrast, deputy managers of large or medium firms generally earned from 23,000 to 29, 000 baht, while the starting salary of a general manager (with 6 to 15 years experience) averaged some 50,000 baht, and in a few large companies, 70,000 baht: pp. 56–57.

[23] Voravidh Charoenloet, "The Shop-House Ready-Made Garment Manufacturing," in Pasuk and Itoga, *Informal Sector*, pp. 38, 41, 48–51.

[24] Ibid., p. 38. see also Pasuk Phongpaichit, "Nu, Nit, Noi and Thailand's Informal Sector in Rapid Growth," in Chira and Itoga (eds.), *Human Resources,* pp. 90, 93–98, 101–3.

[25] Kevin Hewison and Andrew Brown, "Labour and Unions in an Industrialising Thailand" (working paper no. 22, National Library of Australia, 1993) on the fragmentation of the workforce, inhibiting strong organizations of trade unions, pp. 20–21.

[26] Ernst W. Gohlert, *Power and Culture: The Struggle against Poverty in Thailand* (Bangkok: White Lotus, 1991), p. 22. See also Sungsidh, "Labor Relations," *Rat thun*, pp. 309–10.

"In the last five years [the] general labour situation has been peaceful," reports a labor specialist. Nationwide strikes and lockouts had not even reached two digit figures in 1990; but there were 57 wildcat strikes.[27] Such strikes as did occur appear to have been motivated by the desire to gain material improvements, such as higher wages and better work conditions, rather than the decision to assert workers' rights, such as the right to organize. Government officials, for their part, generally give low priority to labor relations. It is only when large-scale strikes break out that officials make an effort to reach a settlement, from fear of "political instability." [28]

As a result of official indifference, there is little pressure on employers to conform to existing, relatively undemanding, labor regulations. "Many of them [employers] are irresponsible in using unfair labour practices, such as bad working conditions, lack of industrial safety, etc." And even though they pay low wages [often below the official minimum wage], employers can still attract workers from the pool of unemployed or underemployed, and from the steady flow of migrants from the countryside. There is, moreover, little pressure on employers to improve their abusive practices, "because the government cannot enforce the law properly."[29]

The strike over textile factory layoffs in July 1993—leading to government intervention to bring back the dismissed workers—put an end for a time to that "tranquil" phase. Since then there have been increases in the minimum wage while earnings in the public sector, especially, have improved. Strikes occur, but sporadically, in specific enterprises.

Moreover, even those economists, among others, who criticized the callous methods of the employers in 1993 (sacking staff without proper consultation and in disregard of years of service, for the sake of rationalizing production) recognize that Thai firms need to make greater use of labor-saving technology (and to upgrade work skills) if they are to compete effectively against lower-wage countries like Indonesia, China, and Vietnam. Thus, the competitive requirements of the economy, on the one hand, and the pool of available labor, on the other, indicate the likelihood that business (and middle class) interests will continue to prevail.

MIDDLE CLASS

Propelled by the rise of business, the middle class is the major constituent of civil society. The thrusting and aggressive "fixer" who deals in money politics represents the brasher, seamier side of the middle class. Yet the fixer is the "client" of wealthier or more powerful "patrons" and at the same time is the patron, or boss, of underlings

---

[27]Nikom Chandravithun, "Labour Administration and Labour Relations in Thailand," in Chira and Itoga (eds.), *Human Resources*, pp. 149–50. See also Kevin Hewison, "Thailand," in Hewison, Richard Robison and Garry Rodan (eds.), *Southeast Asia in the 1990s: Authoritarianism, Democracy and Capitalism* (Sydney: Allen & Unwin, 1993), pp. 173–75, especially on the Chatichai government's conciliatory moves toward the unions. On numbers of strikes and disputes, see Hewison and Brown, "Labour and Unions," table p. 22.

[28] Chira Hongladarom, "The Rise of Trade Unions and Industrial Relations System in Thailand," in Suchart (ed.), *Thailand on the Move: Stumbling Blocks and Breakthroughs* (Bangkok: Thai Universities Research Association, 1990), pp. 183, 186. Government policy, according to Sungsidh, is to weaken the unions in order to maintain competitive conditions in a global economy: "Labor Relations," pp. 329–30.

[29] Chira, "Trade Unions," p. 182. Poorly paid child workers, often from the age of seven, are especially at risk from dangerous work, for example in the construction industry or in small-scale workshops: Nikorn Veesaphen, coordinator for Union for Civil Liberty, in Pasuk and Itoga, *Informal Sector*, pp. 99, 118–19.

who do the actual fixing. Involvement in patron-client relations, a role appropriated by the ascending middle class from the declining aristocracy (and bureaucracy), is one characteristic form of middle class behavior.

The activities and values of Thailand's middle class have facilitated the dual progress of political (democratic) and economic (capitalist) "modernization." A variant of that development is the move from authoritarian to liberal corporatism. Yet another variant (considered deviant from the standpoint of "modernization theory") is the "circulation of the elites," a pattern set into motion when one would-be elite faction attains power with the support of the masses, then acts on its own as an elite, and is in turn overthrown by a new challenger. Marxist and neo-Marxist theories of the middle class (including world system and dependency theories) tend to vary in their portrayal of "the state." In the orthodox Marxist formulation, for example, the state is no more than the "executive committee" of the bourgeoisie; less deterministic Marxists, however, consider the state as the "relatively autonomous" terrain for struggle between capitalist "fractions" and other social forces.

The differences among Thai scholars as to the character and role of the "middle class" furnish an endless subject for current debate. Preecha Piampongsan, for example, queries the adequacy of Western concepts, whether Marxist or Weberian (or "neo-" versions of both), in explaining the emergence, ideas, and activities of the middle class in Thailand. Such theories, he argues, have little relation to reality; they fail to explain the origins of the middle class and what it is. Instead, he contends, understanding class formation in historical terms is more satisfactory. The relationship of the middle class to the rise of capitalism, to state power, and to the workers and peasants, is crucial to this interpretation.[30]

I entirely agree. Hence my conception of the middle class which acts in symbiosis with capitalist development, on the one hand, while benefiting from the erosion of "alternatives" (whether of left or right), on the other. The situation of the "middle class" is complicated, various, even contradictory, and so resists the boundaries typically established by neat theoretical systems. Again, the middle class, although possessing certain behavioral characteristics in common (pragmatism, materialism, individualism), is divided occupationally (from well-paid executives to indigent academics) and by values: according to a greater concern for order or for freedom and justice.

In this latter respect—the concern for freedom and justice—it is only "Modernization theory," of all the variants considered, that corresponds closely to Western-style liberal democracy. All the other theories—corporatism, circulation of elites, and patron-client relations, including "democracy in the Thai style"—are permeated by the concern for order. (Orthodox Marxism, admittedly, is concerned with justice, but hardly with liberal democracy.)

All the same, these theories are not monolithic, but are ambiguous, reflecting the heterogeneity of the middle class itself. Consider patron-client relations, which has both "noble" and "base" implications. The "base" qualities emerge when individuals pursue modern forms of economic or power relations but in a traditional framework, which has long accommodated superior-subordinate relations, the exchange of

---

[30] Preecha Piampongsan, "The Middle Class: Concepts and Theories" (in Thai), in Pasuk and Sungsidh (eds.), *Chonchun klang*, pp. 80–87. In my view, however, it is not a question of exclusively western or indigenous concepts, but of working for a synthesis of the two, as in "area studies."

"services" in return for protection, the formation of a leader's "following," and so on. Modern patronage relations are very much part of the symbiosis of the middle class with economic development.

The "noble" form of patronage is a carryover from the aristocratic virtues of the past, as Niddhi Aewsriwong has formulated so well. The middle class, he argues, understood and even accepted the rules and system of values of the former ruling group (power, honor, and security). Yet the rulers in the past regarded themselves as guardians of the "public good," associating their power with benevolent status (*bun* and *barami*), which the Thai middle class is unable to do. The middle class believes in development and change (contrary to the stability of the old society), but has lost the world outlook basic to democracy (equality, freedom, and the rights of all people). The middle class has modified the old system, without producing something new. Its only basis is money and power.[31]

The "noble" form, by contrast, is a way of making merit, which can be earned through such actions as sponsorship of the deserving poor (to appropriate a Victorianism). Gratitude and loyalty are inherent in such a relationship. Nevertheless, such virtues also sustained (by making it more palatable) the highly unequal relation of power, status, and wealth under the old regime. It is my argument that the middle class, in turn, has both noble and base characteristics; and that NGOs, in particular, and civil society in general express the noble form.

PATRON-CLIENT RELATIONS

Relations between patron and client pervade Thai society from top to bottom, according to many observers. "Thai officials are integrated into a network of patron-client exchange relationships that are at the very heart of the political process. These relationships act as links between state officials and societal groups in business, agriculture, labor, the aristocracy, and the intelligentsia."[32] In regard to the military, factionalism and patron-client relations are directly linked. Factionalism is "inherent within the modern structure of the military establishment because it exercises a patron-client relationship covering nepotism, personal and intermarriage ties, and business and commercial links."[33]

As another writer puts it: "A constantly shifting network of patron-client relationships remains at the base of the authority structure today. Consequently, people think in hierarchical terms; subordinates seek to please their bosses, and people expect to do so and to receive favors. Thai society is rife with this type of behavior, often stigmatized by corruption, as it clashes with the forces of modernity."[34]

Ideally, the patron is akin to the benevolent head of family; in reality, in Gohlert's view, such a relationship results in exploitation and engenders distrust. It is the consequence of long-standing practices: the belief that one's own efforts and contributions do not matter in comparison with those of a powerful patron, who can

---

[31] Niddhi Aewsriwong, "Culture of the Thai Middle Class," in Pasuk and Sungsidh (eds.), *Chonchun klang*, pp. 60–65.

[32] Clark D. Neher, "Thailand," in Neher, *Southeast Asia in the New International Era* (Boulder, Colo.: Westview, 1991), pp. 44–45.

[33] Suchit Bunbongkarn, *The Military in Thai Politics 1981–86* (Singapore: Institute of Southeast Asian Studies, 1987), p. 11. See also Teeranat Karnjana-uksom, "The Military and Business" (in Thai), in Sungsidh and Pasuk (eds.), *Chonchun klang*, pp. 286–87, and types of benefit, pp. 289–91.

[34] Gohlert, *Power and Culture*, p. 18.

assure success; the existence of factionalism, which characterizes all levels and sectors of Thai society; and the resulting weakness of cooperative efforts over extended periods of time, generating little effective pressure to take collective action in response to major social problems. The indifferent attitude of the middle class in Bangkok to the problems of rural society is but one example of this characteristic lack of faith in the efficacy of organized collective civil action.[35]

Patron-client relations, Neher sums up, exist in a society where institutional links (parliament, political parties) are still weak. These relations flourish in a society where there is considerable inequality in property, status, and power. "Little people" need to find a patron; in return for protection and favors they offer their services. Those in high positions must generate enough money (often through corruption) to provide resources and protection for their followers—in order to maintain their loyalty in the competitive struggle between factions.[36]

Nevertheless, in my view, the concept of patron-client relations between superior and subordinate complements, as a social theory or model, but does not replace, a structural analysis of the production and distribution of wealth, power and values in modern society. Modernization theory is one attempt at analysis.

MODERNIZATION THEORY

In a dynamic assessment, James Coleman asserts a positive correlation between political, social, and economic aspects of development. The modernization process is experienced in six major areas:

(1) National identity: the transfer of loyalty and commitment from "primordial groups" to the larger political system;
(2) Political legitimacy: referring to legitimacy of the "modernizing elites" and the authority structures of the new state;
(3) "Penetration": centralization of power; the central institutions of government are the source of final authority;
(4) Participation: development of symbolic or participatory institutions and political infrastructure to channel modern mass demands for a share in the decision-making process;
(5) Integration: the organization of coherent political processes and patterns of interacting relationships for the making of public policy and the achievement of societal goals; and
(6) Distribution: the effective use of government power to bring about economic growth, mobilize resources, and distribute goods, services and values in response to mass demands and expectations.[37] The modernization that results, according to another leading exponent, Daniel Lerner, is manifested by indus-

---

[35] Ibid., p. 80. See also Sompop Manarungsan, "The Middle Class and Thai Agriculture" (in Thai), in Pasuk and Sungsidh (eds.), *Chonchun klang,* on vote-buying and land acquisition through patronage, p. 269; also Sompop Manarungsan, "Alternatives for Agricultural Labor" (in Thai), in Pasuk and Sungsidh (eds.), *Phonlawat thai,* on land speculation, p. 88.

[36] Clark D. Neher, "Political Corruption in a Thai Province," *Journal of Developing Areas* (1977), quoted by Pasuk Phongpaichit, "Gift Cheques and Gin Muang: Corruption and Democracy in Thailand," paper for Political Economy Centre, Chulalongkorn University, 1992, p. 19.

[37] James S. Coleman, "Modernization," in *International Encyclopedia of the Social Sciences* (New York: Macmillan, 1968), pp. 398, 400.

trialization, urbanization, increased incomes, schooling, literacy, and media exposure, and by party membership and voting.[38]

Is that all? Not even the most "modernized" government could claim such "effective" distribution! Evidently, there is a long way to go before modernization (according to such criteria) is operative in patron-clientelized Thailand. More significantly, the consensual implications of modernization theory are debatable. (Coleman's "positive correlation," for instance, is simply taken for granted.) Even the assumption that "modernizing elites" function in a particular way can hardly go unquestioned.

Thus, at one time, the military was prime choice as an "agent of modernization" because of its presumed national organization, social recruitment basis, discipline, unity and "developmental" values. (Development values of a sort have, of course, long been dear to "trading generals.") Currently, the middle class has emerged as favorite: but its establishment of "symbolic or participatory institutions" to channel modern mass demands—let alone "achieve societal goals"—has not gone very far. "Development"—not necessarily democracy—centers the ideology of the middle class. Moreover, bureaucratic authority and an unreconstructed military hierarchy also remain problematic elements in the process of democratization, as can be seen below.

CORPORATISM

Two forms of corporatism, which are more relevant than Modernization theory to development in Thailand, can be distinguished: authoritarian and liberal. Authoritarian corporatism, as practiced for example in Latin America (from the 1960s to 1980s), has a certain affinity with Italian fascism (with or without the ideology of national grandeur). Under the domination of a single party or the military, society is segmented into "functional" groups—peasants, workers, women, youth, professionals, etc.—each of which, under co-opted leaders, exercises a certain limited autonomy. The leadership of each functional group is responsible both for "representing" the group within the overall corporate structure and at the same time for keeping order within the group. Authoritarian corporatism presents a powerful, and readily coercive, hierarchical structure of authority from top to bottom.

Nevertheless, Thailand's bureaucratic polity, in its heyday, could not really be considered as an example of authoritarian corporatism, simply because the extra-bureaucratic social forces were either too small and weak (there were few independent professionals) or too cowed (workers and peasants) to need "co-opting." But in the present transitional phase between the decline of the bureaucratic polity and the potential ascendance of a "bourgeois polity" it could be argued, as Anek does, that a "liberal" form of corporatism is emerging.

> Liberal corporatism is marked by a high degree of autonomy and spontaneity, and by the central role of private groups in the creation and operation of their representative associations, as well as systems of government-group interest mediation. . . . [Indeed] organized business has formed politically effective extra-

---

[38] Daniel Lerner, "Modernization," in *International Encyclopedia of the Social Sciences* (New York: Macmillan, 1968), pp. 387, 389.

bureaucratic groups and the policy of the government is no longer determined solely by the bureaucratic elite.[39]

At the present stage, however, only business has been brought into some kind of corporatist arrangement with government—in particular with technocrats in administrative departments and government-linked agencies. So far from consolidating this arrangement, the Chuan government took a more laissez-faire attitude toward business and neglected the "joint public and private sector" committee favored by bureaucrats under Prem. Indeed, economists like Rangsun and Medhi point to the continuing crucial role of governmental technocrats in formulating economic policy, especially in regard to fiscal controls.

Such macro-economic policy (in the corporatist style) is largely insulated from political and traditional bureaucratic pressures, being managed by technocrats (in the Ministry of Finance, Bank of Thailand, Budget Bureau, and other agencies) who adhere to the virtues of fiscal conservatism, as Scott R. Christensen points out. Politicians, excluded from this area, rely on sectoral allocations instead (quotas and tariff exemptions, price subsidies, contracts and concessions). This "soft-authoritarian model" is pragmatic in that it accommodates such interests and, to some extent, also accommodates pressures from the military, while at the same time carving space for technocrats and business elites to manage Thailand's export-led economy. But the corporatist model is primarily Bangkok-based; its success is "confounded" by the political articulation of the urban-rural split.

Moreover, other functional groups, as Anek points out, are by no means accorded the autonomous status of business. Peasant cooperatives are "hierarchically organized and closely supervised by the government," and the "internal operation and leadership selection" of trade unions are "under close official supervision." It is precisely this uneven process of development that results in continuing tension between the authoritarian institutions in society, even if they are in decline, and the more open politics of the last decade, with its multiparty system and competitive general elections, which are conducive to the liberal form of corporatism.[40]

CIRCULATION OF ELITES

Pareto's famous, or infamous, theory of the "circulation of elites" is an important alternative to the theories so far considered in at least three respects: it presents a cyclical, and not unilinear, political process; it emphasizes emotional drives ("sentiments") which are later rationalized in a logical form; and it argues that, except for short periods of time, people are always governed by an elite. History, in Pareto's view, is an incessant struggle between elites.

"The greater parts of human action," Pareto asserts, "have their origin, not in logical reasoning, but in sentiment." It is only later that people invent logical principles to justify their actions. "The people who are carried away—usually unknowingly—by these currents [of sentiment] and who . . . wish to represent involuntary acts

---

[39] Anek Laothamatas, *Business Associations and the New Political Economy of Thailand: From Bureaucratic Polity to Liberal Corporatism* (Boulder, Colo.: Westview, 1992), pp. 13–14. See also Medhi Krongkaew, "The Economics of Institutional Change: The Private Sector and the Making of Economic Policy in Thailand" (1994), also citing research by Rangsun Thanapornpan. See also Scott R. Christensen, "Capitalism and Democracy in Thailand," paper for Association of Asian Studies conference (Washington, D.C., April 1992), pp. 8–9, 18–20, 31–34.

[40] Anek, *Business Associations*, pp. 155–61.

as voluntary and non-logical actions as logical ones, conjure up strangely imaginary reasons, which they use to try to deceive themselves as well as others about the true motives of their actions."[41]

In this way, a newly emerging elite, with "energy and strength on its side," strives to replace the existing elite, but does not admit its intention openly. Instead, it declares in emotional terms that it pursues the good of the people in general. Once it wins power, it either subjugates its former allies, or offers formal concessions. Yet this new elite cannot last; it will, in turn, be overthrown by a younger and more vigorous challenger drawing on emotive appeals to the humble and weak against the rich and strong.[42] How many within the elite, Pareto declaims, invoke "immortal principles," giving imaginary causes to their acts while concealing the real ones?[43] In this way the Thai elite can be seen to stir up similarly primordial passions of patriotism and sacred traditions—"nation, religion, monarchy"—in order to defend itself from the subversive threats of socialism and pluralist democracy.

It is, of course, doubtful that "socialism," which Pareto predicted (and feared) would be the watchword of the new elite, will play that role at present. But even if it did, in Pareto's Machiavellian view, this would not make much difference. For once they had seized power, the socialists, like previous elites, would simply turn against their supporters—or co-opt their leaders—and ignore the interests of the masses. (Undeniably, this was the case in Soviet Russia and elsewhere.) Pareto recalls the way in which the revolutionary doctrine of Christianity had triumphed, subjectively, that is, in terms of the relations between psychological states. But objectively—in terms of the relations between "real objects"—he was convinced that there will still be rich and poor, powerful and humble, and new brothers will continue to betray fellow brothers, even a thousand years from now.[44]

Pareto's brand of realism is unfashionable, and his sweeping assertions may seem implausible, but his insistence that government (whatever the apparent form) represents rule by an elite cannot be evaded. The tendency, even in the West, to form a separate caste of "professional politicians" isolated from their constituents is already evident.[45] As for politicians from developing countries, the watchword of "democracy" may well conceal, Pareto-style, the challenging ambitions of the middle class elite.

Marxism and the Bourgeoisie

Marxism shares with Modernization theory—the rival "other"—a certain "automaticity," a faith in the "inevitable" correlation between economic developments and political results: for Marxism, the rise of the bourgeoisie is followed by the collapse of

---

[41] Vilfredo Pareto, *The Rise and Fall of the Elites: An Application of Theoretical Sociology* (Totown, N.J.: Bedminster Press, 1968, orig. 1901), pp. 27, 35.

[42] Ibid., pp. 36, 41.

[43] Ibid., p. 35.

[44] Ibid., pp. 27, 37.

[45] See, for example, Pierre Bourdieu, *Language and Symbolic Power*, edited by John B. Thompson, translated by G. Raymond and M. Adamson (Cambridge: Polity, 1991). The formation of the "monopoly of the professionals" in the political field is achieved by competence in training, apprenticeship, and practical mastery of the immanent logic of politics. Political parties constitute the "rules of the political game"—a game exclusive to the initiates and not to the uninitiated, that is, "the people" who choose their politicians: pp. 171–72, 176, 179–80.

capitalism; for modernization, economic growth results in the triumph of democracy (for Pareto, the triumph of a new elite).

Judged from the orthodox Marxist standpoint, the democracy advocated by Modernization theory is a sham: the institutional facade behind which lurks capitalist exploitation. There are, however, problems with this conception. Most seriously, the prediction of the inevitable disintegration of capitalism as it matured (from the ripening of inherent contradictions) has not come about; rather, it is its opposite, communism, that has collapsed.

Now, the implausibility of Marxism's fundamental assumption about capitalism also casts doubt on the theory's derivative assumption about democracy. Thus, most Western Marxists now recognize that liberal democracy is not a mere facade, but provides essential safeguards for human rights and individual freedoms that are threatened by authoritarian and totalitarian regimes alike.

Orthodox Marxism does, however, acknowledge (along with Modernization theory) the "renewing" impetus on traditional society of the rising bourgeoisie. But although both theories posit the establishment of the "bourgeois polity" as a goal, the way to achieve it remains uncertain. The same critique applies, I suggest, to such variants of Marxism as "world system" theory and dependency theory. The former, by its overwhelming concentration on the "system," marginalizes the "parts" of the system, that is, particular countries, especially when they are confined to the "periphery." Dependency theory, too, allows no autonomy to indigenous developments. According to its pronouncements, the "national bourgeoisie" is a fiction, while the autonomous establishment of capitalism is impossible. The Thai situation clearly refutes such dogmatic assumptions, as Hewison and others have pointed out.

Is there, then, no case for Marxism? Although its "prescriptive" search for a proletariat and a bourgeoisie continues—to some effect in Thailand—the value of the prescription itself is somewhat dubious. All the same, Marxism as a "critique" remains a valuable tool of analysis, notably by differentiating people and groups as they relate to such a fundamental "institution" as the production and distribution of wealth in society.[46] For the structure of wealth—and of power and the value-system—is fundamental to any study of questions concerning national renewal by civil society.

CIVIL SOCIETY—AND THE ROLE OF NGOS

INTELLECTUAL TRANSITION

Works of intellect and culture are the supreme expression of civil society: they have an important, if often indirect, effect on both elite and popular attitudes toward the economy, politics, and social problems of "development."

Modern Thailand has an intellectual tradition that goes back to the early decades of the century, inspired by such diverse personalities as Pridi Panomyong, the civilian leader of the 1932 "constitutional" revolution; Prince Wan, who linked the old regime and the new by his tireless creation of neologisms (derived from Sanskrit and other sources) to provide "Thai" concepts for the modern world; and the remarkable

---

[46] A good discussion of critical Marxist scholarship in the political economy journal (*Warasan setthasat kanmuang*) is in Hong Lysa's contribution to Manas Chitkasem and Andrew Turton (eds.), *Thai Constructions of Knowledge* (London: SOAS, 1991), pp. 102–12.

purveyor of culture, information, and political insight, Kukrit Pramoj, who incarnates the transition from bureaucratic authoritarianism to a more open political system.

No less important, among cultural figures on the left, were the socially committed writer, Kularb Saipradit, and the brilliant Marxist intellectual, Jit Phumisak, whose mocking deconstruction of Thai "feudalism" stimulated the student rebels of the 1970s. It is significant, however, that even such prominent student leaders of the "October Revolution" as Thirayut Bunmee and Seksan Prasertkul have become recognized academics; they realize that the heroic period is over and (like their former opponents) that Thailand has entered a new age dominated by economic growth and the hesitant process of democratization.

It is in this "middling" situation—neither authoritarian nor revolutionary—that another line of intellectual development can be traced, starting from Pridi, founder of Thammasat University and author of the first comprehensive "Plan" of development by a political leader; continuing by way of Pridi's disciple, the technocratic but humanitarian Puey Ungpakorn, who was for a time Rector of Thammasat; and culminating in the upsurge of non-governmental organizations (NGOs)—the very spirit of civil society—in which one of Dr. Puey's sons is a leading figure.

Pridi's Plan, produced in 1933, evokes the Buddhist sentiment of compassion for the plight of the poor, especially in the countryside, and of the need for action that animates many of the present-day NGOs (although the prescribed action is very different). As Pridi writes of the poor:

> Sympathy springs up unbidden at the sight of their inadequate food, clothing and shelter, the bare necessities which are all they have in life. Even when they have food for today, tomorrow and the days after tomorrow are unpredictable. The future is at best precarious. When one considers the uncertainties of life, the way in which we are all subject to old age and disease, one may well ask whether those who, while they are still well and strong are so poor and needy, will in such eventualities have even food to eat.[47]

Pridi's remedy, however, was state ownership of the land (private enterprise is "wasteful") with the transformation of peasants into salaried workers. "There is no better method than government control of the economic system"—but the transformation would be brought about through cooperation between rich and poor, and the use of legal methods. "It is true that there will be less freedom of a sort," Pridi admits, "but the loss in personal liberty will be more than compensated for by the general increase in the happiness and prosperity of the people as a whole."

The Plan is a system "by which we can press forward to this golden age. . . ." The Plan was considered "communistic" by the conservative leaders and, although Pridi himself was cleared, it was never revived. Pridi, leader of the "Free Thai" movement, which backed the Allies during World War II, was for a short period Prime Minister. He fled after the 1947 military coup, spending the rest of his life in exile.

Puey, at one time Governor of the Bank of Thailand and the first director of the Budget Bureau, in turn participated in, and thus represents the technocratic transition to economic growth and efficient "national development," but in an era of

---

[47] Translated text in K. P. Landon, *Siam in Transition* (1939), quoted in D. Insor, *Thailand* (London: Allen & Unwin, 1963), pp. 80–82.

authoritarian rule. Puey was no narrow materialist, however; he inspired many of the younger generation by his concern that "the fruits of economic growth should be shared more equitably by people in the urban slums and rural areas." Moreover, Puey encouraged planners and economists to apply Buddhist precepts to the development process. In the early 1970s, he inaugurated a rural development project by three major universities, using interdisciplinary approaches to tackle the problems resulting from rural poverty. Puey's projects (as Rapin notes) became models for NGO work from the 1980s.[48]

It is this basic concern for those who do not benefit from official development policies, or who are actively discriminated against by powerful officials or wealthy businessmen, that motivates the "third generation"—that of the NGOs. Unlike the first generation, inspired by an outstanding political leader (Pridi), or the second generation (such as the humane technocrat Puey), the third generation specifically reflects the emergence of civil society, inspired by the challenging task of "renewal."

The most significant forces pressing for "renewal" originate from political parties, academe, and religious, environmental, and rural development advocacy organizations. The potential for renewal is generated, in effect, at three levels: through exemplary personal leadership, at the top; through institutional responsibility for more effective expression of social issues, for example, among professionals and political parties, at the intermediate level; and through "grassroots" work, especially the work of NGOs.

Renewal mirrors the development of civil society itself. When "voluntary" groups and associations, independent of the state, begin to "profess" their group character and identity, they "affirm their allegiance" to specific sectoral norms.[49] This is the first stage in the formation of civil society. The second stage transcends a purely corporate identity and envisions society as a whole as well as the roles of groups and individuals within it. "Profession" then means "openly declaring" a conception of society *as citizens*—a conception which is not necessarily adopted by the controllers of the state or of business interests. The third stage is the realization of that conception: that is, to "profess" in the third sense—to "perform the duties" required by the new situation.

DEFINING THE AGENDA

Members of the academic "profession" have had an important influence in Thailand over the last two decades, not so much by directly shaping the political process (although the short-lived Chatichai government's "brains trust" did play such a role) as by helping to define the public agenda. Here is one example—a significant one— of academics "speaking out" on the social agenda that they professed.

At issue, during the May 1988 elections, was whether the prime minister should be an elected member of parliament or could be unelected, like the incumbent prime minister Prem. (The same issue was to surface again, in a far more traumatic fashion, in 1992.) Public opinion polls had shown that 80 percent of respondents wanted an elected prime minister, in accordance with democratic principles. The military, how-

---

[48] Larry D. Stifel (1984), quoted by Rapin Quinn, Australian National University doctoral thesis on the role of Thai NGOs. See also Puey Ungpakorn, *Glancing Back, Looking Forward* (Melbourne: Shepparton Press, 1975), on the failure of the orthodox belief that the benefits of economic growth would "filter down" to the poor.

[49] "Profess": to affirm allegiance; openly declare; perform duties (of a profession), etc.: *Concise Oxford Dictionary*.

ever, backed Prem's candidature. Indeed, the threat of military action was implicit—
it became explicit four years later—in the statement by the army commander-in-chief
that the army was powerful enough to launch a coup, but only if the public decided
on that course of action. It was in an atmosphere of crisis that ninety-nine prominent
citizens, mostly academics, spoke out in their petition to the king:

> Political confusion [affecting] the people's faith in the parliamentary democratic
> system is increasing with each moment. Division and disunity have occurred
> among the military, civil servants and the people because the political leader
> who is caretaker head of the government has not been truly neutral. He has
> allowed the military forces . . . to be used as a show of force to support personal
> political status. This has led to unnecessary divisions. . . . We do not agree with
> changes outside of the legitimate rules, especially coups d'état, and are ready to
> sacrifice personal benefit for the country to have justice, peace and order, happi-
> ness and a voice and participation by the people. . . .[50]

After the election, Prem voluntarily stepped down, and Chatichai as the elected
head of the largest political party then became prime minister. As Ockey points out,
the group of ninety-nine had indeed altered the agenda of discussion, shifting the
terms of debate from a show of force (on behalf of Prem) to the need for neutrality
and the principle of an elected head of government. A military coup, in such a
context, would clearly be illegal. Indeed, as the petitioners had demonstrated, it was
the threat of action by the military that was now causing "division" in Thai society,
not the constitutional protest by citizens: a reversal of the traditional (bureaucratic
polity) argument.

It was under very different circumstances—when the Chatichai government had
alienated much of its original public support—that the military, under new leadership, staged its February 1991 coup. But the attempt, more than a year later, to install
the unelected army chief Suchinda as prime minister provoked that extraordinary
demonstration by members of civil society which was to result in the humiliation of
the military leadership.[51] Three years later, the king's inspiring address in July 1995,
proclaiming the democratic virtues, including the need for an elected prime minister,
set the seal of royal approval on the constitutional separation of powers.

But time and commitment are needed to "institutionalize" what was a spontaneous outburst of "people power." According to democratic theory, this is achieved
through the deepening involvement of political parties throughout the country, with
the genuine aim of representing the interests of their constituents.

---

[50] Reported in *Bangkok Post*, May 27, 1988: quoted by James Soren Ockey, "Business Leaders,
Gangsters and the Middle Class," PhD dissertation, Cornell University, Ithaca, New York,
1992, p. 356.

[51] The core of the demonstrators in May 1992 was made up of middle-class professionals,
executives, and administrators. Nearly half those surveyed by the Social Science Association of
Thailand were employed in the private sector. (Another 14 percent were self-employed, while
students were under 9 percent.) More than 45 percent of the demonstrators surveyed earned
lower-middle or middle-class incomes; Anek Laothamatas, "Sleeping Giant Awakens: The
Middle Class in Thai Politics," paper for conference on the democratic experience in Southeast
Asian countries, Thammasat University, December 1992. Text of the king's insistence in July
1995 on the need for good government and support for "legitimacy" (in English) and the
democratic virtues: *Matichon sudsapda*, August 22, 1995.

THE PARLIAMENTARY PROBLEM

Representation of the interests of citizens is the proclaimed task of political parties and parliamentary government. And it is significant that a new generation of politicians is now bringing a more professional spirit to an assembly still dominated by parochial interests. But parliament as a whole is still inadequate to its task. Besides the lack of commitment to the "general interest" that parliamentarians are also supposed to represent, there are two further serious defects in parliament.

The first, as Ammar and Christensen have emphasized, is that acts of parliament typically have little policy content. They allocate enormous authority to subordinate legislations controlled by permanent officials and cabinet ministers. Moreover, "this administrative discretion is assigned to departments rather than ministries, so that an already fragmented State is further balkanized." In addition, "many laws and subordinate regulations have little to do with genuine economic development activities, and often they reflect little more than agency-based deals cut among officials from different departments and between officials and private citizens." Indeed, "Parliament as an institution has little authority or interest to scrutinize the activities of the bureaucracy."[52]

Genuine reforms, as these analysts conclude, are few and far between in the Thai body politic. Instead, and this is the second major defect of the "semi-democratic" system, parliamentarians are mainly interested in opportunities for self-enrichment and personal advantage, resulting in incessant intrigues and faction-fighting for lucrative ministerial positions; they are also engaged in paying back (for votes) their predominantly rural constituents, by channeling public resources and thus building up patronage networks in their home provinces.[53] (For a review of the interaction of government and political parties since the restoration of parliamentary government after mid-1992, see the following chapter.)

In view of the disappointing performance of the party system, it is from sources *outside* the bureaucracy and an ineffective parliament, in civil society, that the impetus for reform and renewal is most evident. The outspoken role of the press, the renewal of Buddhism, the challenge of the environment, and the movement for "empowerment" in the countryside: these are significant sectors of change. Yet they are not without weaknesses—most conspicuously in the case of the media.

MEDIA CONTRASTS

In comparison with the relative independence of newspapers, such as the large-circulation *Thai Rath* and the business-oriented *Phujadkan*, and the influence (through the 1980s) of Kukrit's political and social commentaries in *Siam Rath*, for example, radio networks and television stations have long been subjected to close bureaucratic (especially military) control. "The radio news which was networked nation-wide," as Pasuk and Baker point out, comprised "a succession of press-releases by military and government departments . . . on the importance of national security, and the role of the army in society and politics."

As for television:

Until the mid-1980s, the news on all four channels amounted to a daily reaffirmation of the political hierarchy. It began with court news, followed by reports on

---

[52] Christensen and Ammar, *Beyond Patronage*, p. 14.

[53] Ibid., pp. 16, 36–38.

the activities of the prime minister, head of the armed forces and other political figures in strict pecking order. The army channels regularly ran short messages on the importance of the army in society.[54]

The contrast between the passivity of state-controlled radio and television and the courageous stand of the newspapers (notably the English-language *The Nation*) was impressively demonstrated during the May 1992 crisis, when radio and television were forbidden to cover the massive protests against the Suchinda regime and only the press revealed what was really going on.

Intellectuals, as Voravidh reports, substantially helped the movement of resistance by giving interviews, making proclamations, carrying out debates, and writing newspaper columns. They emphasized that the May 1992 demonstrations were a direct result of the military coup of February 1991, which threatened the basic rights and freedoms of the people. "Professors for democracy" and members of the liberal professions played a key role, often as eye-witnesses, in informing the public.[55]

The press has certainly flourished since 1992 and, with the Philippines press, is the most free in Southeast Asia. Some large-circulation newspapers have played an important role in exposing corruption and other forms of political or social abuse. Investigative reports in *Thai Rath*, for example, revealed the Phuket land reform scandal which in 1995 brought down the Chuan government. Not to be outdone, its rival in the circulation battle, *Khao Sod*, reported the scandalous misconduct of the famous monk, Phra Yantra, who, too, was forced to resign.

Problems, however, remain (besides the relentless outpouring of sensation, sex, and scandal). One is the attempt by "dark forces" (godfathers or other influential people) to prevent press disclosures affecting their interests. (*Thai Rath* claimed, for example, to have been threatened in August 1995 following its reporting of police promotions, personalities and motivations.) Another holdover from the past is distorted or biased reporting, prevalent among the larger papers. But even the well-regarded TV program *Mong tang moom* ran into criticism in the run-up to the July 1995 elections. The moderator asked some loaded, but justifiable, questions concerning the reputation of certain Chart Thai leaders, while letting the Democrats (afflicted by the land reform scandal) off the hook. Some months later, the Banharn government, stung by continuing media criticism of corrupt practices, banned the program.

Buddhist Renewal

The leading political role of Chamlong, charismatic former general and devout Buddhist, who became a major protagonist in the May 1992 crisis, is a striking illustration of Buddhist renewal. In addition, the influence of "alternative" Buddhist thinkers and movements, and the Buddhist "character" of the government's amnesty to students and others who "entered the jungle" after the 1976 coup, are no less significant instances of Buddhist-inspired challenges to traditional attitudes. I shall start in reverse order.

---

[54] Pasuk and Baker, "Towards Civil Society," *Thailand: Economy and Politics*, p. 375. The contract for a private-sector TV channel was, however, awarded in 1995.

[55] Voravidh, "The Middle Class and May 1992," in Sungsidh and Pasuk (eds.), *Chonchun klang*, pp. 122–23.

Prime Minister Kriangsak's amnesty policy, introduced in the late 1970s, was one of the contributing factors in the collapse of the insurgency, as noted above. Kriangsak had himself seized power from the rigidly anti-communist Thanin government in reaction to the latter's divisiveness and inefficiency. Kriangsak sought to return to a more balanced, pragmatic course internally and externally (seeking détente with communist Indochina). Bringing back Thai radicals students from the jungle into society fitted the same conciliatory strategy. It was certainly an astute political move. But it also reflected, it could be argued, humanitarian feelings inspired by a Buddhist outlook. Whether this is so or not, the peaceful (and largely unharassed) return of "forest fighters," who had been calling for the armed overthrow of the government, was a remarkable achievement by any standard.

The second example of renewal derives from the student-led democracy movement in the early 1970s, which transformed formerly passive "subjects"—factory workers, peasants, village monks among them—into "participants." This process, however uneven, has gathered momentum in the following two decades: perhaps all the more so because of the perceived weakness of political parties in the context of military assertiveness and capitalist expansion, with its concomitant corruption.

In voicing this need for participation, the well-known Buddhist scholar and activist, Sulak, denounced the February 1991 coup leaders in no uncertain terms:

> None of their actions since the coup has been legitimate, and they have shown no sign of wanting to work for social justice for the country and the people or to pave the way for liberty, fraternity, and equality. There has been no move towards a liberal democracy. The trend has been to secure more power for themselves by increasing the military budget . . . while ordinary people are becoming poorer and more oppressed.[56]

Another writer has argued that the current revivalism among alternative Buddhist movements marks "a turning point in the history of Thai Buddhism." The past two to three decades has been a "dynamic period in Thai Buddhism, involving changes in all major aspects, namely, doctrinal interpretations, the *vinaya* rules of the monks, the roles of laymen, the establishment of Buddhist communities, and the incorporation of high technology in the propagation of Buddhist messages."[57]

Such changes have arisen under conditions of intensive economic development, giving rise to the formation of a Thai middle class, consisting basically of professional people, owners of small private businesses, and lower ranking civil servants. In contrast to the villagers, who have been the major followers of traditional Thai Buddhism, members of the middle class are better educated, economically better off, and more exposed to the mass media. They are also the main adherents of three major Buddhist movements outside the traditional mainstream.[58]

Buddhadasa, one of the most original and creative Buddhist thinkers, represents the first movement. Radically, he reinterpreted the karmic law (the cycle of births and rebirths) to cover a moment in *this* life—not indicating only past lives. This inter-

---

[56] Sulak Sivaraksa, *Seeds of Peace: A Buddhist Vision for Renewing Society* (Berkeley, Calif.: Parallax, 1992), p. 128.

[57] Suwanna Satha-Anand, "Religious Movements in Contemporary Thailand: Buddhist Struggles for Modern Relevance," *Asian Survey*, April 1990, p. 396.

[58] Ibid.

pretation, as Suwanna points out, can be subversive of the traditional justification of a person's high status as due to accumulated merits in previous lives. Indeed, Buddhadasa's concern with social and political reforms has been greatly admired by Thai intellectuals.[59]

A second group attempts to cater to the religious needs of the urban masses in a very different way. The Dhammakaya movement provides a meditative practice which for believers promotes a happy state of mind, and their gratitude is shown by payments in cash. The total assets of the movement, with its related real estate business, has been estimated at well over one billion baht. The "mass marketing of religious pleasure" is certainly relevant to contemporary Thailand.[60] Indeed, market values have compromised the behavior of such well-known monks as the former Phra Yantra, who fled to the United States, and Luang Pho Pawana, whose sexual promiscuity titillated readers of the press in 1995.

The third Buddhist movement is the most contentious: Santi Asoke. In its reformist austerity it is directly critical of the materialist indulgence both of new (such as Dhammakaya and other wealthy foundations) and traditional Buddhism. Santi Asoke "attacks the capitalist consumer culture that has created many social ills, which have as their root cause the excessive and expanding desire for material goods."[61] But the most socially challenging feature of Santi Asoke is the insistence of its founder (Phra Photirak) on independence from the established Buddhist hierarchy—resulting in persecution by the civil and religious authorities—and the activity of the most famous of his disciples, Chamlong.

The milieu in which politically active Buddhists have emerged over the past three decades is well described by Somboon: "Political repression, peasant misery, social injustice and political crises are demonstrated [in his book] to explain the ideological stands, responses and policies of the political monks."[62] These monks actively participated in the democratic movement of the early 1970s as well as in support of particular peasant demands, such as the call for land redistribution. It was dissatisfaction with the existing socio-economic and political structures that motivated them. They concluded that the Sangha (clerical organization) was not only undemocratic and corrupt, but also served to legitimate the existing state and its bureaucratic institutions.[63]

Indeed, and this is the third aspect of Buddhist renewal, Chamlong's own · ethical-political career parallels the stirring of these hitherto quiescent monks. For Chamlong was one of the founders of the "Young Turks" movement in the army, whose experience of rural conditions in their combat role (fighting the communist

---

[59] Seri Phongphit (1982), writing on the Dhamma and Politics, quoted by Peter A. Jackson, *Buddhism, Legimation and Conflict* (Singapore: Institute of Southeast Asian Studies, 1989), p. 126. Jackson has written an intellectual biography, *Buddhadasa—A Buddhist Thinker for the Modern World* (Bangkok: Siam Society, 1988). The import of Buddhadasa's thinking can be seen in such works as *Thamik Sanghkomniyom* (Dhammic Socialism) and *Prachathipatai baeb sanghkomniyom* (Social Democracy), both published in 1974.

[60] Suwanna, "Religious Movements," pp. 400–402. See also Jackson, *Buddhism*, on access to the "Buddhist market-place," pp. 116–17, 200–219.

[61] Suwanna, "Religious Movements," p. 404; see also Jackson, *Buddhism*, pp. 160–70.

[62] Somboon Suksamran, *Buddhism and Politics in Thailand* (Singapore: Institute of Southeast Asian Studies, 1982), p. 9.

[63] Ibid., pp. 55, 65–66, 83–90, 101–2, 105–12, 163–67.

insurgency) made them realize the urgent need for social and political reforms. As one of their leaders explained:

> The Young Military Group was born and became actively engaged in politics amidst the 14 October 1973 crisis. Since then . . . we were forced to be involved in politics. For we could not let national security remain in the hands of those dirty politicians or even senior officials in the Army who are irresponsible to the nation and allowed themselves to be subservient to the rotten political system [in response to material benefits].[64]

Chamlong himself withdrew from active membership of the Young Turks and instead, by the late 1970s, became a strict follower of Phra Photirak. He was appointed by Prem to the key position of Secretary-General in the Prime Minister's Office, and he sided with Prem in the 1981 coup attempt.[65] Two years later, however, Chamlong boldly opposed the attempts by the army leaders to intimidate the political parties into prolonging the constitutional amendments (empowering the military-controlled Senate). "I am speaking up because I cannot stand the threats of certain military officers," he bluntly declared. "I cannot stand by to see democracy destroyed. The atmosphere has changed in a way which shows who is on the side of democracy and to unmask those who wish to have dictatorship."[66]

Chamlong's austere personal life, his repudiation of corruption, and his commitment to democracy mark the stages of a remarkable career: from his dramatic victory as elected Governor of Bangkok in 1985 (re-elected in 1989), his foundation of *Palang Dharma* (moral force) party, and his courageous defiance of Suchinda and the military in the May 1992 demonstrations. *Palang Dharma* was represented in the Chuan government coalition, but Chamlong at first stood aside from ministerial politics, preferring to set a moral example of disinterested and progressive social purpose. He changed his mind a year later, accepting the post of deputy Prime Minister; he was instrumental in the collapse of the Chuan government (over the land reform scandal) in 1995. Faction-fighting within the Palang Dharma party and Chamlong's authoritarian behavior, however, have seriously tarnished his image.

ENVIRONMENT

Undoubtedly, the attractions of material consumption, which Chamlong was striving to overcome, do exert a strong influence on values, affecting newly affluent urban elites and increasingly consumer-oriented villagers. Ecologists argue that these West-

---

[64] Col. Manoon, secret address to the Young Military Group, June 27, 1980, quoted by Chai-Anan Samudavanija, *The Thai Young Turks* (Singapore: Institute of Southeast Asian Studies, 1982), p. 31. See also his report on the background of members, pp. 27–30; and on the need to counter socio-economic and political injustices, pp. 58–61.

[65] Jackson, *Buddhism*, pp. 182–83.

[66] *Bangkok Post*, February 8, 1983, quoted by Ockey, "Business Leaders, Gangsters," p. 380. See also Sombat Chantornwong, *Wiwatanakan lae naeonom khong phakkanmuang mai: syksa chapo karani phak phalang tham* [Evolution and trends of new political parties: a case study of the Palang Dharma party] (Bangkok: Foundation for Study of Democracy and Development, 1989), on Chamlong's experiences, pp. 14–15, 22–24, 29; the problems of the people of Bangkok and their revulsion from money politics, pp. 18–20; on Santi Asoke, pp. 16, 31, 34, and the attacks on it, pp. 52–53, 56; on Palang Dharma, pp. 28–30, 35–38, 46–47, and the need, in Sombat's view, to limit the influence of Santi Asoke on the party, p. 56.

ern influences are often harmful to the environment, contrary to supposed Buddhist values about living in harmony with nature. There is, indeed, growing recognition that the quality of life and the health of people and of the environment are suffering as a result of Thailand's headlong rush to development.[67]

One significant attempt to provide an alternative is the community development movement in rural areas aimed at "sustainable agriculture," which is supported by Buddhist leaders, NGOs, and environmental groups. Such local communities, with the support of other groups, have had some success in resisting environmentally damaging development projects, designed to benefit domestic elites and foreign interests. The World Bank, for example, has (at last) been persuaded to refuse funding for several large dams proposed by the Electricity Generating Authority of Thailand. Moreover, protests against eucalyptus plantations (displacing villagers and creating environmental problems) have been widespread.[68] Yet the return of commercially motivated ministers in the 1995 Banharn government does not augur well for environmental safeguards.

Indeed, for decades the environmental impact of government-supported "economic development" had been almost totally neglected. (It was only the catastrophic floods in South Thailand in 1988, resulting in many deaths, that forced the then Chatichai government to ban the illegal logging that had greatly contributed to the disaster.) Such reckless deforestation has reduced the forest cover from three-quarters of the country in the 1930s to less than one-third in 1985 (and only 10 percent in the river headwaters, where protection is vital). Deforestation is caused both by large-scale commercial exploitation (often by businessmen with influential political connections) as well as by encroachment of landless peasants.[69]

Excessive use of pesticides in agriculture, a practice widely promoted by commercial firms, further damages the environment by poisoning rivers, fish and irrigated areas. Water pollution both by industry and by urban households is especially serious in the Central Plain, with consequences for Bangkok's own water resources. Of course, the pollution (and traffic congestion) of the capital is notorious. (According to United Nations statistics, published in August 1995, Bangkok is the most polluted city in the world—ahead even of Mexico City.)

The sheer concentration of manufacturing industry in and around Bangkok has resulted, on the one hand, in the metropolitan region—with ten percent of the population—producing nearly half the country's GNP. At the same time, the inability of government and bureaucratic agencies to agree upon or to enforce planning controls

---

[67] Helen Ross and Suwattana Thadinitti, "The Environmental Costs of Industrialisation," paper for conference on "The Making of a Fifth Tiger?: Thailand's Industrialisation and Its Conseqeunces," Australian National University, December 1992: Principle of Sustainability, sec. 6.

[68] Ibid., sec. 7. On the so-far successful challenge to a proposed dam in Surat Thani, where village and urban opposition was mobilized by university students, see Prudhisan Jumbala and Maneerat Mitprasart, "Mobilization Movement Formation and Politicization: Environment-Related Cases from Southern Thailand," paper for fifth international Conference on Thai Studies, London (SOAS), July 1993.

[69] Anat Arbhabhirama et al., *Thailand Natural Resources Profile* (1989), quoted ibid., p. 3. See also Philip Hirsch, *Development Dilemmas in Rural Thailand* (Singapore: Oxford University Press, 1990), p. 39 on illegal timber traders promising poor, often landless farmers a piece of land in forest reserves if they cooperate in logging operations.

has aggravated congestion and pollution in Bangkok.[70] Such lopsided development has had even more serious consequences for the countryside.

RURAL DEVELOPMENT

Thailand has had a remarkable record of economic growth over the last three decades (of which Bangkok is both material beneficiary and environmental victim). But in the countryside, where some two-thirds of the people live, the population has received an ever-decreasing share of the nation's wealth. (Agriculture's share of GDP is now less than 12 percent.) In addition, the land itself is unequally shared: the top 16 percent of farmers operate 44 percent of land, while the lowest 44 percent of farmers operate only 13 percent of land. This is not to mention increasing numbers of landless laborers.[71]

Admittedly, as a result of overall economic growth and an effective population policy, the proportion of people living in poverty has markedly declined from about two-fifths in the 1960s to about one-fifth today; yet the total still amounts to nearly twelve million people. Nearly 90 percent of these are villagers, both farmers and agricultural laborers. The rural poor, as one specialist points out, tend to have larger families and fewer income earners compared to the non-poor, and their education levels are much lower. Most of them also lack such basic amenities as toilet facilities, piped water, and electricity.[72]

Moreover, income inequality is worsening, and this particularly affects the countryside because of "bias in policy implementation toward favoring industrial over agricultural activities, favoring large over small business, and favoring urban over rural people."[73] As another economist states:

> Government policy relating to rural development failed to achieve its objectives because it [has] been determined in an urban context. The government spent very little on rural development—some 6 percent of the entire national expenditure budget—and enforced policies which effectively brought down the income

---

[70] Ross and Suwattana, "Environmental Costs," p. 6. According to a United Nations report in October 1993, Bangkok's dust levels in 1989 were estimated to have cost 28 million lost work days and to have contributed to 1,400 deaths. Average lead blood levels are already four times the U.S. standard. A number of mass transit plans are in various stages of development to ease traffic jams and alleviate pollution; but their implementation has been delayed again and again by changes in government and by infighting among politicians and bureaucrats: reports from Bangkok, *Straits Times*, October 23, 1993. [The king was openly incensed about this situation, speaking out in 1993 and especially in 1995: see the next chapter.]

[71] Andrew Turton, "Thailand: Agrarian Bases of State Power," in Gillian Hart, Andrew Turton, and Benjamin White, *Agrarian Transformations: Local Processes and the State in Southeast Asia* (Berkeley: University of California Press, 1989), quoting the agricultural census in 1978: p. 58.

[72] Pranee Tinakorn, "Industrialization and Welfare: How Poverty and Income Distribution are Affected," paper for "Fifth Tiger" conference, pp. 3, 4, 7.

[73] Ibid., p. 12. The income share of the top 20 percent of the population increased from 49 percent in 1975 to nearly 55 percent in 1988; that of the bottom 20 percent diminished from 6 percent to only 4.6 percent (table 7). The Northeast has by far the highest incidence of poverty (more than one-third of the total), with the South and North each accounting for about one-fifth, and the Bangkok region only 3.5 percent.

of farming families and further widened the gap between rural and urban people.[74]

On the one hand, rural areas have indeed benefited by improved access to hospitals, better communications, electricity, new roads, and some curbs on the influence of middlemen. But there is also a "dark side": improved access to the village has opened the floodgates to consumer goods on hire-purchase (contributing to growing indebtedness), to commercialized agriculture, environmental problems, the erosion of indigenous culture, and the rise of powerful local elites.[75]

Moreover, relations are often tense or conflicting among the four main groups in the countryside: (i) small farmers or landless peasants (the poor), who comprise some 20–30 percent of the rural population; (ii) the middle farmers, well-to-do, proving agriculture and accumulating capital, who form as much as 50–70 percent of the population; (iii) agribusiness and large farmers, perhaps 5–10 percent; and finally (iv) those with "influence" in the countryside, such as traders, millers, transporters, who act as political and economic intermediaries between villagers and the wider world. The crucial role in future development, as Pasuk points out, is that of the middle farmers. They demand higher budgetary allocations and crop price supports (contrary to industrial interests, which seek lower food prices), and it is to their advantage to develop stronger links with major political parties.[76]

Sompop likewise draws attention to the "static" character of much of present-day agriculture, and to the problems of lower rice prices, increasing competition for land, and persistent areas of poverty. It is important for farmers to move out of rice production (which still claims about half of all cultivated land) and to diversify into cultivation of vegetables and fruit, other cash crops, and stock breeding. Above all, the creation of farmers' organizations is essential for them to play a more effective role, both by encouraging alternative agricultural methods and by influencing government policies, which have so long been biased against agriculture.[77]

It is in combating the urban bias of official policies and redressing, whenever possible, the consequent abuses that NGOs have been most motivated. Although they have achieved some striking successes (as well as many mixed results), at last the efforts of a small number of sincere and well-intentioned people can have but a

---

[74] Prayong Netyarak (1988), quoted by Gohlert, *Power and Culture*, p. 21. Taxes and export quotas, reluctance to act against monopolies, and subsidies to industry in the Bangkok region have played a considerable part in creating urban/rural disparity: p. 105.

[75] Ibid., p. 23. An official meeting organized in 1984 by the Canadian International Development Agency and the Thai Department of Technical and Economic Cooperation noted the lack of community participation, uncertainty as to land tenure, the unstable market system, and lack of social consciousness in the bureaucracy as major failings: ibid., p. 104.

[76] Pasuk Phongpaichit, "Farmers, State and Capitalists" (in Thai), in Pasuk and Sungsidh (eds.), *Phonlawat thai*, pp. 37–40, 54–64. Moreover, many small farmers do not benefit from the government policy of directed credit, because only about half the cultivated land is covered by "acceptable" land titles: Christensen et al., *Thailand: Underpinnings of Growth*, p. 16.

[77] Sompop Manarungsan, "Middle Class and Thai Agriculture" (in Thai), Sungsidh and Pasuk (eds.), *Chonchun klang*, pp. 249–71; as for "contract farming," although it introduces more predictable economic relations, it requires heavy investments and in itself is no solution for poverty, pp. 260–67; see also Sompop Manarungsan, "Alternatives" (in Thai), in Pasuk and Sungsidh (eds.), *Phonlawat thai*, pp. 71–88; and Medhi Krongkaew, "Contributions of Agriculture to Industrialisation," "Fifth Tiger" conference, pp. 31–32. (Note that the premium tax on agricultural exports was, however, abolished in 1986.)

small impact on the nation because of the sheer scale of the problem. More controversially, perhaps, NGOs have come to accept that it is only realistic to cooperate with government officials in improving the process of development—and proposing alternative ways—rather than (as in the past) directly confronting officialdom.[78]

The NGO thesis can be summarized in this way:

(1) Problems of development—poverty, ill-health, low education, etc.—are inter-related.
(2) Governments are not in a position to provide all the services that people require.
(3) People have a right to be involved in seeking solutions to their problems.[79]

An experienced NGO worker and analyst crystallizes this thesis in four concepts: basic needs, people participation, self-development, and human rights.[80] Rapin explains the variety of experiences, ideas, and formulations at work. Following Alain Touraine, she emphasizes the need to open a political and cultural space for social actors, rather than relying on the old-style attempts to seize control of the state. Further, she advocates a positive re-evaluation of Buddhism (as opposed to the radical critique that defines Buddhism as a mere instrument to be manipulated by the state). It follows that the role of NGOs is, first of all, to try to understand the pattern of social interaction in a period of rapid change; and second, to understand the power structure and system of production—rather than dismissing or opposing it categorically—and then to work out alternatives.

Yet an important question remains. To what extent have NGOs either collaborated with or been obstructed by officials in tackling outstanding social and economic problems, in enabling villagers to become self-reliant, and, above all, in helping the poor and marginalized, who are victims both of the development process and of the parallel political process? In both cases, they are increasingly subject to the sway of local elites, operating at an intermediate level in the overall structure of power and wealth. Does this situation seriously compromise their effectiveness?

---

[78] The first major gathering of NGOs in 1981 agreed (though not unanimously) that "coordination with government agencies is necessary," despite the "suspicious attitude of government officials towards NGOs": Gohlert, *Power and Culture*, p.34.

[79] Ibid., p. 52. A further alternative is the "community culture" approach. See Chatthip Nartsupha, "The Community Culture School of Thought," in Manas and Turton, *Thai Construction of Knowledge*, on the work of NGOs, the importance of Buddhist principles (righteousness, subsistence, balance with nature, communal life), and the significance of anarchism in Thai life: pp. 118–38. A convincing defense of the movement against Jonathan Riggs's strictures (*World Development*, 1991) is by Kevin Hewison: "Nongovernmental Organizations and the Cultural Development Perspective in Thailand," *World Development*, vol. 21, no. 10, pp. 1699–1706. Community culture is distinguished from orthodox development by its populism, conservatism, and "overly romantic" character, but this may be as much a strength as a weakness. See also Chatthip and Siraphon Jidathan, "Villagers" (in Thai), in Suwanna Satha-Anand and Nuangnoi Boonyanate, *Kham: Rongroi khwamkhid khwamchya thai* [Words: key terms in Thai thoughts and beliefs] (Bangkok: Research Division, Chulalongkorn University, 1992), pp. 219–28.

[80] Rapin Eiamlapa, "People's Participation and the State: A Study of the Role of Non-Governmental Organizations (NGOs) in the Thai Development Process," MA thesis, Australian National University, Canberra, 1990, introduction.

Structural imperatives are still the determining factors guiding the government's priorities and actions; hence the official emphasis on economic growth rather than equitable distribution. Despite greater awareness of rural problems (because of their potential for social unrest) there has been "no fundamental restructuring" of the bureaucracy, as Hirsch puts it. For the most part, he concludes, official groups stifle local initiative, work to rigid bureaucratic standards, and provide unresponsive leadership.[81]

NGO attitudes towards the government are accordingly ambivalent. On the one hand, cooperation (as noted above) is seen as the only practical way to help ordinary people increase their economic productivity: an attitude the government favors, because it provides a role for NGOs within the framework of national development. On the other hand, NGOs also seek to exert countervailing power so as to work out a new consensus with the government: a role that the latter does not favor, and which it even regards as a threat or challenge to government authority.[82]

The resulting "political sociogram" of the Thai development community (Gohlert's expression) is that of an independent set of players, with varying degrees of influence, but dominated by government agencies. The power wielded by the public sector is conventional in nature: it is derived from the traditional authority of the state as opposed to influence flowing from the community. Such community participation as exists generally translates into forms of cooperation with local elites, who facilitate (and derive most benefit from) the work of government agencies. "Natural or formal leaders, village committees and community organizations already in place, tend to be the contacts and channels for program implementation."[83]

The dark side of development is precisely the rise of these "local powers" who exploit their intermediary status—between people and bureaucracy, and between people and the capitalist sector—for their own ends. (Note the section on "Money Politics" in the previous chapter.) In Turton's findings, these "local powers" form a small minority of village households (perhaps 5 percent), but possess a degree of wealth, control of resources, prestige and power which sets them apart from the majority. Among the influential people are the better-off landowners, commodity dealers, shopkeepers, village officials (headmen and district chiefs), rice-millers, moneylenders, owners of small-scale transport and machinery concerns, the larger employers of wage labor, and so on.[84]

Their process of accumulation is multi-faceted (it includes illegal operations), but especially involves direct and indirect government patronage. It includes privileged access to low interest credit, to state-owned land (enabling the recipients to establish plantations in forest reserves), as well as access to official budgets for development projects and to infrastructural improvements. In sum, such local powers are crucially dependent upon—and provide an essential link between—the capitalist sector (beyond the village) and the state bureaucratic sector.[85]

---

[81] Hirsch, *Development Dilemmas*, pp. 21–22, 188–89.

[82] Rapin, "People's Participation," pp. 128–29.

[83] Gohlert, *Power and Culture*, pp. 35, 57. See also Banthorn, "NGOs and Thai Democracy" (in Thai), in Sungsidh and Pasuk (eds.), *Chonchun klang*, especially on the "rights" and the "development" NGOs, pp. 311–19.

[84] Andrew Turton, "Local Powers and Rural Differentiation" in Hart, Turton, and White, *Agrarian Transformations*, p. 82.

[85] Ibid., pp. 81–83.

Wealth and power accumulated in this way are further enlarged by the very process of economic—and political—development. Thus, large sums are spent by local elites on establishing and maintaining social relations with strategic superiors and subordinates in order to enhance their status, secure lucrative offices and contracts, and accumulate more political and economic clients. They also go into politics, at the district or province level, and are thus articulated in a "complex overlapping of economic, political, administrative and cultural agencies, relations and interests" with the "power bloc" of the state.[86]

It is in this complex, difficult, and even dangerous terrain that NGOs operate. (The murder in July 1995 of a small-farmer organizer in the Northeast, triggered by his opposition to an environmentally damaging enterprise backed by a political figure, shows the length to which "local powers" will go.) And yet, precisely because official attitudes are so often obdurate and one-sided, and because local power structures play such a privileged part (at the expense of the powerless), NGOs play a crucial role in Thailand. As Rapin expresses it:

[NGOs] address in particular the economic, social and political problems of the poor such as the low price for paddy and uncertain prices for other cash crops, the condition of slum dwellers [usually migrants from the countryside], the exploitation of child labour and child prostitution as well as the political and legal disadvantages suffered by the poor. The ultimate aims of the NGOs are not only to combat suffering but also to raise people's consciousness and to propose political and legal reform through social welfare and structural-analysis [investigative] approaches. Their activities include the distribution of goods and income to the poor, assistance in the control of productivity, and help for the people to gain power to determine their own destiny.[87]

Rapin and other analysts are candid, however, about the besetting weaknesses and even failures of NGOs: notably, lack of coordination, factionalism, top-down attitudes (similar to those of the bureaucracy they criticize), small-scale capacity, and lack of wide public support. Nevertheless, as Gohlert emphasizes: "Their principal human resource is increasingly professional and highly committed people, generally from a middle class background, who share explicit humanist values."[88]

To conclude this brief report: defense of human rights, grass-roots politics, and people's participation are indispensable and inseparable. It is only through their linkage in civil society that independent and self-reliant communities can emerge, protecting the people from abuse of power and helping to improve their livelihood:

---

[86] Ibid., pp. 83, 86–88. Again, refer to "Money Politics" in the previous chapter, and to Sombat Chantornwong, "The Role of Local Godfathers" (in Thai), in Sungsidh and Pasuk (eds.), *Chonchun klang*, pp. 119–37, especially on the opportunities for the *jao pho* as a result of economic development, on the one hand, and democratization, on the other.

[87] Rapin, "People's Participation," p. 111.

[88] Gohlert, *Power and Culture*, p. 114; on NGO limitations, pp. 56–57, 63, 107, 114, 116. See also Rapin, "People's Participation," on lack of experience, irregular financial support, and difficult domestic climate: p. 158; and concrete examples, pp. 166–69.

"A representative regime is not only the goal but also the means for the people to achieve a better and peaceful society."[89]

---

[89] Ibid., pp. 120–21. Kevin Hewison and Garry Rodan emphasize the role of NGOs in building opposition coalitions among trade unions, development groups, women, religious bodies, and environmentalists (i.e., members of civil society). Above all, they can maintain an intellectual life, creating space for debate (1993 paper).

4

TWIN PEAKS—DISTURBING SHADOWS[*]

ECONOMY, POLITICS, SOCIETY IN THE 1990s

The twin "peaks" of achievement in Thailand are economic growth and democratizing uplift, which according to modernization theorists go together. The "shadows" cast by the twin peaks refer, on the down side, to the social consequences of rapid industrialization and the political consequences of the spread of capitalism. From a combination of these two features, three connected themes emerge: the narrow and contested scope for political action in dealing with economic and social problems; the subversive effect of "money politics" on the democratizing process; and the challenge of (non-elected) technocratic "efficiency" to parliamentary representation, with its frequent lack of coherence.

Two significant events—the disastrous fire in 1993 in the Kader toy factory and the "Anand affair"—illustrate the importance of these themes. Finally, in the context of this complex pattern of "assets" and "liabilities," there is the ongoing interaction of economic and political forces: government policies and opposition reaction, the military stance, labor and rural concerns, infrastructure and the environment, civil society (including human rights) and foreign affairs.

The "peak" of economic growth—amounting to over 8 percent increase in gross domestic product in 1994 and in 1995—was aided by high domestic demand and a stable political climate resulting in increased foreign investment. Despite the looming current account deficit, there has been a high rate of savings and exports are booming, although inflation may be difficult to control.

Yet, despite the remarkable record of economic growth (averaging from 7 to 8 percent a year throughout the 1970s and 1980s), economists are concerned about continued high government spending, which has been implemented partly to overcome social problems, spending that is likely to increase inflation and add to the current account deficit. In addition, underlying problems, such as a shortage of skilled labor (resulting from secondary education deficiencies), infrastructure bottlenecks and water shortages need to be tackled in order to stimulate future investment. Failure to improve Bangkok's traffic "gridlock" and the adverse effects of water shortage for agriculture and industry remain serious problems.

A major *social* consequence of consistently high growth rates over the last three decades is that the Thai "middle class" has doubled since 1970, so that it now comprises about one-fifth of the employed population; this is not far short of the

[*] John Girling, adapted from "Twin Peaks," *Southeast Asian Affairs, 1994* (Singapore: Institute of Southeast Asian Studies, 1994). I am grateful to Julaporn Euarukskul and to Rapin Eiamlapa Quinn for their help in updating this piece.

urban working class (some 22 percent in 1989). Conversely, farmers (and family labor), which in 1970 made up more than three-quarters of the workforce, now constitute less than half, while the number of landless laborers has grown significantly (to nearly 9 percent).[1] Such socio-economic changes have had a substantial impact on Thailand's "transition" to a more open but also far more unequal society (60 percent of the people share less than one quarter of the national wealth) with the rise of "money politics" and consumerist values.

The terrible fire at the Kader toy factory in May 1993 revealed the harsh side of economic achievement: that is, the social cost of Thailand's headlong rush to industrialize. Nearly two hundred workers were killed, mostly young women, and hundreds more were injured in the worst factory fire in modern history. The factory, in Nakhon Pathom near Bangkok, was not equipped with a fire alarm or proper fire escapes, and the factory construction was "substandard," according to the province police chief. Labor experts (quoted by the *Nation* on May 13, 1993) said the blaze demonstrated that Thai safety standards lagged far behind the country's rapid economic growth. Officials admitted that besides large factories (such as Kader's), small-scale sweat-shops abounded, where owners were intent on squeezing maximum profits from their workers and could rely on virtual immunity from official inspection.

In a nationwide check of some 30,000 factories following the Kader fire, police safety inspectors found that more than 60 percent lacked fire alarms. In many factories, emergency exits and windows were blocked. In Bangkok, more than half the factories checked had no fire alarms; two-fifths had no proper fire extinguishers, and nearly the same proportion had no emergency exits. As for worker compensation in the Kader fire, the firm at first offered only a third of what the government considered to be reasonable, and only after pressure was applied did it offer anything approaching the official amount. (The firm's headquarters are located in Hong Kong, and the company itself is controlled by Hong Kong and Taiwanese investments and linked to the wealthy CP conglomerate, as part of a global toy-making industry.)

The dark side of economic growth was exposed by the Kader fire. The conditions of the workers in that tragedy were in many ways typical, characterized by low wages and lack of safety precautions. These low-wage workers tend to be migrant women who labor long hours in poor conditions, helping to make Thai exports competitive. Workers typically have very little influence on safety conditions, because of their lack of bargaining power (and the weakness of trade unions in general). Moreover, according to labor specialists in the Ministry of the Interior, there

---

[1] Report of Labour Force Survey, National Statistical Office, cited by Pasuk Phongpaichit and Chris Baker, "Jao Sua, Jao Poh, Jao Tii: Lords of Thailand's Transition," paper for 5th International Conference on Thai Studies, London, SOAS, July 1993. See also the interesting paper by Richard F. Doner and Ansil Ramsay, "Competitive Clientelism and Economic Governance: The Case of Thailand" where the authors seek to account for the country's economic success (leading to the emergence of the middle class) despite a fragmented polity and without a strong (disciplined, efficient) state. Their explanation, broadly, is that elite rivalries have been conducive to a competitive rather than monopolistic economy; clientelism—relations between business and ruling elite—through various institutional arrangements has also produced, when needed, a collective response to threatening economic conditions; and official macroeconomic policies have been insulated from sectoral (especially political) pressures: chapter in Ben Ross Schneider and Sylvia Maxfield (eds.), *Business and the State in Developing Countries* (forthcoming).

were only fifty safety inspectors who were supposed to enforce fire regulations at some 90,000 factories.

The second "exemplary" event was the "Anand affair," which besides exposing partisanship in the judiciary also brought out the wider issue of technocratic efficiency versus equitable parliamentary representation (admittedly sullied by factionalism and incompetence). Early in 1993, a disgruntled, now-retired judge sued Anand Panyarachun, the former caretaker prime minister, for allegedly blocking his promotion. The verdict in the criminal trial against Anand and his associates is still pending, following a series of perhaps deliberate procedural delays. (At one stage "a happy ending" was expected after the mediation of a "high-level" person, but so far this has not materialized.)

The importance that the key terms of this protracted conflict took on—legal autonomy versus administrative intervention, and the reformist drive versus judicial "cronyism"—roused strong feelings on both sides. Significantly, professional support for Anand—the "good man" wrongly under attack—demonstrated the revival of "civil society," after the heroic days of May 1992. On the other hand, a senior judge (of the Office of Judicial Affairs) blamed the "Friends of Anand" for stirring up public emotion, which he claimed could "make the public lose faith in the court system" and even lead to the unraveling of Thai society. Social critics, however, insisted that time was long overdue for the reform of the judiciary, which had become the last stronghold of conservatism (as it granted legitimacy, for example, to military coups).

The wider significance of the Anand affair, however, is that it brings up once again the controversial question that asks the nation to weigh the efficiency (and integrity) of Anand's technocratic regime against the accountability of elected government—accountability offset by the undoubted corruption of the previous (Chatichai) government and the dubious reputation of "unusually wealthy" ministers in the Banharn government. The remarkable reforming record of the Anand administrations—marked by bold decisions on important projects, greater "transparency" intended to combat corruption and reduce monopolistic tendencies, and even an effective "poll watch" scrutiny of elections—certainly provides a contrast with the imperfect record of the political parties in office.

Yet it must be remembered that the Anand administrations were "caretaker" governments: they had no independent life of their own. Moreover, they were made possible only by the military coup of February 1991—even though Anand in many cases clearly demonstrated his independence of the military. Such a technocratic regime, in other words, illustrates one feature of the "authoritarian-developmental" model in which certain successes (Soeharto's in Indonesia, and those of the military leaders up to—but not after—1987 in South Korea, for example) are more than counter-balanced by failures elsewhere. But technocracy versus democracy need not be a zero-sum game. It is quite possible for a well-organized government to draw strength from both.

This is, indeed, what Anand himself has suggested.[2] The question is no longer whether to opt for economic development or for democracy, he argues; they must proceed together. From one point of view, Asians have no experience of democracy or democratic culture, so economic development must be given priority in the short

---

[2] Keynote speech, February 18, 1993, Asian Institute of Management, Manila, reported by the *Nation*, February 19, 1993.

and medium terms. But another view, the former prime minister went on, is that Asians are so closely integrated with the outside world, and share so many of its political, social, and economic expectations, that democracy is the only form of government that can provide the requisite political and social underpinnings for human rights, material well-being, and progress.

Each point of view produces its own cultural mindset, as Anand puts it. Economic development without democracy has the propensity to lead to authoritarianism; but democracy without economic development is inherently unstable, for undue emphasis on political freedom without due regard for performance, and the responsibilities of performance, could give rise to dangerous irresponsibility and license. Moreover, failure to deliver the "economic goods" could spark challenges to the legitimacy of democracy itself.

Economic efficiency and administrative integrity are, indeed, the "technocratic" virtues. But the question remains (unanswered by Anand): under what kind of alliance can the technocrats display—or be allowed to display—these qualities? The developmental concerns were evident when the technocrats worked under Sarit—but their democratic concerns were not so evident. Elements of both were favored during the Prem administrations, but the democratic experience was severely constrained by the prior needs of the state and business. The democratic liberalization under Chatichai was in turn undermined by the prevalence of money politics. Only under the "cautious" Chuan (1992–1995) has something of a balance been achieved between democracy and development.

What the noted human rights campaigner, Gothom Arya, said of the Anand court case is equally appropriate to this wider political issue: "We should respect the independence of the judiciary [read: the authority of the technocrats]. But what about its accountability? More and more, the Thai public is speaking in favor of having both."[3]

* * * *

To repeat: the "shadow" on the peak of economic achievement is the social cost of rapid industrialization and urbanization; and the paradox (for democratic theory) is that an enlightened technocracy may be more capable of social reform than an elected government, vulnerable to powerful pressure groups.

The second related paradox is that the more open society resulting from economic and social "modernization" also provides more opportunities to make money (legally or illegally) and more opportunities to exercise the power of wealth—a development that leads to the corresponding decline of bureaucratic authority. (Note the provincial example of a recent survey in Khon Kaen where not one government official was identified as being "politically influential," in contrast to a big businessman, a prominent "godfather," and the local MP, who were.)[4]

---

[3] Quoted by Tan Lian Choo, Bangkok correspondent of the *Straits Times*, April 30, 1993. See also Ammar Siamwalla, President of the Thailand Development Research Institute, "The Dilemma Facing Thailand's Reformers," *Business Times*, February 3, 1993; and Chai-Anan Samudavanija, "Industrialisation and Democracy in Thailand," paper for conference on "The Making of a Fifth Tiger?" Australian National University, December 7–9, 1992.

[4] Survey results cited in Kevin Hewison and Maniemai Thongyou, "The New Generation of Provincial Business in Khon Kaen: Economic and Political Roles," paper for 5th International Conference on Thai Studies, pp. 17–19. See also Sombat Chantornvong, "Local Godfathers in

In this context of capitalist expansion and political uncertainty (for democratization is subject to contradictory pressures, from members of civil society, on the one hand, and from a still resentful military and from business, on the other) amid a growing divide between rural and urban Thailand, how have the elected governments fared?

One test of government effectiveness was suggested by Chuan himself, in his 1993 New Year message, when he announced that government priorities would be rural development, the decentralization of administrative power, and a more equal income distribution. "The progress made in these areas," he claimed, "will determine the success or failure of my administration."

On the one hand, the Democrat-led Chuan government was committed to legality and to social reform. On the other hand, the land reform scandal that brought down the government in 1995 is evidence that even a leader of recognized integrity could not overcome corrupt tendencies within his own party. Indeed, Chuan himself was widely criticized for his caution and indecision and for his inability to manage and control his squabbling coalition partners to the detriment of the public good.

Hence the perception, particularly among the inhabitants of polluted and traffic-congested Bangkok, of an inactive and incompetent government, preoccupied with sectional interests and factional rivalries, muddling through a series of crises. Note, however, the view of the well-known economist and former Rector of Thammasat University, Krirkkiat Pipatseritham, who considered—from a wider perspective—the government's record to be "quite satisfactory," judging by the way it maintained economic growth and ensured peace and order. Its efforts to redistribute the national wealth were creditable, even though the results—especially in rural areas—would take time.[5]

Although the personal qualities and the political experiences of Chuan and his successor Banharn could hardly be more different, both governments faced very similar tasks: politically, to hold together the fractious coalition against the intrigues and assaults of the opposition; administratively, to attempt decentralization of the highly centralized and hierarchical Ministry of the Interior, and to clean up the police force (commonly viewed as particularly prone to corruption); to scale back the powers of the military, without provoking armed reaction; to improve working conditions and support trade unions, without antagonizing business; to alleviate poverty and redress rural grievances; to meet environmental concerns, especially pollution and deforestation, without impeding economic growth; to promote human rights, without overstepping the bounds of regional consensus; and to maintain good relations within the region and beyond. These are all vital issues, and are discussed in turn.

POLITICS

The first political fact is that factionalism, which impedes policy coherence and action, has characterized both the "angelic" parties of the Chuan coalition and the "devils" of the then opposition and later of the Banharn government. Perhaps most disillusioning was the effect of factionalism on the Palang Dharma (moral force) party. While its former leader, Chamlong Srimuang, at first remained outside the

---

Thai Politics," paper for 5th International Conference on Thai Studies, on the importance of economic opportunities and electoral competition in furthering the role of godfathers.

[5] Krirkkiat, interviewed by *The Nation*, October 24, 1993.

Chuan government, tension mounted between the purists associated with the Buddhist Santi Asoke movement and the pragmatists under the multi-party veteran, Boonchu Rojanastien. Boonchu later resigned, and Chamlong, head of the religious wing, regained control of Palang Dharma in September 1994. Bitter faction-fighting continued after Chamlong joined the government as deputy prime minister. By early 1995 the party was split into two irreconcilable factions, as leading dissidents, including former Foreign Minister Prasong and former Communications Minister Winai, assailed Chamlong's "disgraceful" management. After defecting from the Chuan government in principled protest against the land reform scandal, however, the Palang Dharma party—under the new leadership of one of the richest men in Thailand, Thaksin Shinawatra[6]—found no problem in joining ministers with dubious records in the Banharn government!

Equally riven by factionalism was, and is, the well-funded, right-wing Chart Thai party that headed the opposition to Chuan and benefited in 1995 when Chuan fell from grace. While Chart Thai's old leader, Pramarn Adireksan (tainted by the charge of being "unusually wealthy") was eventually pushed aside by the ambitious (and very wealthy) Banharn Silpa-Archa, the younger generation also persistently sought a return to the lucrative advantages of office. It was then that faction-fighting was renewed in the struggle for cabinet positions, as discussed below.

Similar enticements of office had their effect on the Social Action Party, whose leader, Montri Pongpanich, was also one of the "unusually wealthy." When Montri, and others, were cleared of financial wrongdoing on a technicality (the military-backed "assets examination" committee was judged to be unconstitutional) he acted with such disdain for the Democrat-led government he had joined in 1993 that the reluctant Chuan was compelled to dismiss the party—which then had to await Banharn's election success to return to office.

An even more tortuous route to power was followed by Chavalit (head of the New Aspiration party) and Interior Minister in the Chuan government, who was also involved in 1993 in a bizarre secret negotiation with the opposition—as he later admitted. ("I know that this kind of thing has been going on the whole year through," was Chuan's resigned comment.) Whether Chavalit was seeking to improve his leverage within the government, as he implied, or was planning to head a new coalition, as opposition leaders suggested, was not entirely clear. Such ambiguity, deliberate or otherwise, had become typical of the former army commander turned politician. In contrast to his past maneuvers, which earned him a reputation as a master strategist, even Chavalit's well-intentioned plans—especially to reform the police—were confused, bungled, or ran into trouble.

Chavalit (and his party) finally defected after two troubled years in office, regaining power and renewing his controversial reputation as Defense Minister in the Banharn government. Contrary to the precedent set by Chuan, Chavalit imposed his own candidates for military promotion in 1995, ignoring the recommendations of the Army Commander-in-Chief Vimol.

To many observers, Chart Thai's 1995 election victory and the appointment of senior ministers with disturbing records was an even more controversial feature of the political scene. The Research Centre of the Thai Farmers Bank estimated that up

---

[6] Details of Thaksin's personal wealth were reported in *Matichon sudsapda*, August 15, 1995. They were revealed by the Palang Dharma party in an effort to force disclosures by other politicians.

to 17 million baht had been spent on the elections by all candidates (purchases included "buying" MPs from other parties). The massive extent of vote-buying surprised even the experienced PollWatch organization, set up (originally by Anand) to supervise elections.[7]

Thirayuth Boonmee, director of the Thai Study Research Institute at Thammasat, for example, criticized the Interior, Health and Justice ministers as being either objectionable to the public or ineffective at their jobs. The majority Therd Thai faction of Chart Thai, in particular, represented a return to the "godfather" type of operation of provincial politics (and lacked a national outlook).[8] This faction claimed that Banharn had promised its leader, Narong Wongwan, a position as head of the Interior ministry prior to the elections. (Narong, however, and another faction leader, Vatana Asavahame, had previously been refused visas to enter the United States, allegedly because of drug trafficking charges.) To avoid further dissension, Banharn himself was obliged to take on this important ministry, for a time.

CONSTITUTIONAL REFORM

As for reform, some progress may have been made as a result of the Chuan government's priority plan for decentralization. Although Palang Dharma's attempt to ensure the election of provincial governors foundered on opposition within Chuan's Democrat party and Chavalit's New Aspiration party—the major elements of the first coalition—a bill to provide more powers to sub-district (*tambon*) councils was approved in November 1993. Nevertheless, only a small minority of wealthier councils would be entitled to sign contracts and raise funds for development purposes.

But more significant was the defeat a year later (owing to Chavalit's defection to the opposition cause) of constitutional articles that had been accepted by the appropriate parliamentary commission and the Chuan government. According to these articles, all local administrative councils would be elected (not appointed), thus undercutting the crucial "vote-collecting" role of village headmen and sub-district chiefs.

Signs of reform did, however, eventually emerge from the convoluted proceedings of the "charter review committee"; the charter they proposed was intended to amend or replace the military-imposed constitution following the February 1991 coup. One of the proposed changes was to replace the appointed Senate (currently dominated by active permanent officials, especially in the armed forces) by a Senate with members allocated according to the number of seats won by political parties at the general elections. "We need to revive public faith in the Senate," the respected academic, Kramol Thongdhamachat, commented. Despite a turbulent year, with party calculations prevailing over democratic commitments (the opposition parties joined hands with appointed Senators against some of the most important changes), in February 1995 the amended Constitution was put into force. The number of Senators was to be reduced to two-thirds of that of the lower house, the voting age

---

[7] Commented Suvit Suvit-Swasdi: "Money politics has become an integral part of Thai society. Influential and ambitious individuals would do anything possible to enter politics—a shortcut to power and riches." *Bangkok Post*, August 6, 1995.

[8] Thirayuth's commentary in *Matichon*, quoted in *Bangkok Post*, August 6, 1995. Nevertheless, the inclusion of the successful businessman, Thaksin, and the experienced administrator, Amnuay Viravan, head of the newly formed Nam Thai party, are assets.

was lowered from twenty to eighteen years, and an election commission is to be established.

Further moves for political reform arose from Banharn's 1995 campaign promise that if elected he would work on the reform guidelines proposed by the Democratic Development Committee, set up under the Chuan government and chaired by the eminent medical specialist and community adviser Prawase Wasi. Indeed, Banharn was impelled to take up this popular cause (if only verbally) in order to offset the damaging effect on urban public opinion, as well as on military, administrative civil service, and business leaders, of certain of his appointments.

The crucial problem, however, was that if the committee to reform the constitution was only composed of experts (that is, largely professionals) and not politicians, it would alienate the politicians; indeed, the latter argued with some justification that they (and not academics) were experienced in politics and knew what could be done. The professionals, on the other hand, reaffirmed the original guide-lines, pointing out that politicians (judging by their record) could not be trusted to produce reforms that were not to their personal advantage.[9]

Nevertheless, the House of Representatives has become more professional (and business-oriented), if not necessarily more progressive. In the previous parliament, more than one hundred members (nearly one third of the total) had BA degrees, seventy had an MA, and nineteen had PhDs. The then House Speaker, Marut Bunnag, in particular praised the well-prepared initiatives of younger members, which are improving the quality of parliament. (A group of young Democrats, mostly professionals, was prominent on the government side; but they were well matched by young opposition deputies, who effectively exposed government misdemeanors.) Yet the parliamentary tone is still set by older members, who are preoccupied with ways to keep their constituents happy and lack a national perspective, according to critics.

Corruption

Prime Minister Chuan had pledged, in his 1993 New Year statement, that he would not allow corruption to degrade his government—and thus provide the pretext for a military coup, as in 1991. In particular, he warned the police to put an end to their own corrupt practices.

An analysis conducted by the Political Economy Centre of Chulalongkorn University pointed to the police department as the most plagued by corruption of all

---

[9] The present system, dominated by rural vote-buying, is clearly unsatisfactory, as Anek Laothamatas points out. Parliament is little more than a rubber stamp for the executive. Moreover, the huge costs of maintaining extensive patronage networks encourages corruption and creates pressures for frequent power shifts: Anek Laothamatas quoted in *Far Eastern Economic Review*, June 29, 1995. As Anek points out in a further interview, the Banharn government, elected by rural voters, is not supported by Bangkok voters, who dislike the combination in the countryside of patronage, money-politics, and dishonest politicians. Nevertheless, for effective political reform, the middle class should try to understand the point of view of people in the countryside and their relative poverty, which makes them susceptible to electoral corruption; and it should encourage rural development, education, and cooperation: see interview (in Thai) *Siam Rath sapdavijarn*, October 1–7, 1995. Opposing viewpoints on the political reform proposals, including opinions of party members from Palang Dharma, Democrat, and Prachakorn Thai , and Democratic Power for Political Reform (Gen. Saiyud), were expressed at a Roundtable Discussion: report in *Sunday Post*, August 6, 1995.

the state organizations. A representative survey by the Centre—of more than 2,000 respondents—also showed that the police department was perceived to be the most corrupt, followed by the defense department, interior (in charge of police, land department, etc.), communications, and so on. As for political parties, Chart Thai was singled out (by more than half the respondents) as the most corrupt, followed not far behind by Social Action (nearly 40 percent); at the other end of the scale were New Aspiration (under 10 percent), Democrats (less than 5 percent) and Palang Dharma (2.6 percent).[10]

The ten "unusually wealthy" politicians were prominent figures in the opposition to Chuan—and several returned to power under Banharn. Their demands for the return of seized "assets"—ranging from more than 600 million baht in the case of a former minister of commerce to former communications minister Montri's 336 million and Chatichai's 226 million and below—provided much scope for political speculation. The Chuan government finally agreed, in conformity with court findings, to return the assets.

Chuan sought to strengthen the rule of law throughout the country. Interviewed in December 1994, he emphasized the need for equality before the law, but admitted the difficulty in enforcing the law effectively. From his own experience of twenty-five years in politics, he also agreed that vote-buying was on the increase, especially because of the greater role of businessmen in politics—a view amply confirmed by the July 1995 elections.

An example of business-political manipulation was the stock exchange scandal that erupted over share manipulation by business people connected to important politicians. (Some 30 billion baht had been spent to raise the price of shares from 10 to 250 baht.) Criminal charges were filed in April 1993 against some thirty persons, one of whom was well known for his links with the military and as a financier of Chavalit's New Aspiration party. (Yet another was related to the former leader of the Democrat party.) The then Finance Minister Tarrin Nimmanhaeminda was praised for his courage in acting against such influential figures "with extensive political connections." Yet in December 1993 police decided not to prosecute in one of the cases of manipulation, because of "insufficient evidence"; it was feared that the others charged, who had cheated small investors out of millions, would be unlikely to go to court because they had the "right political connections."[11] One of the major suspects, and eleven of his associates, were indeed acquitted in June 1994.

Meanwhile, the Phuket land reform scandal shows that where money politics rules even the instruments designed to help the poor and landless can be used to the advantage of the rich and powerful. Investigations by *Thai Rath* in November 1994 had revealed that a large amount of valuable land had been obtained under the amended land reform program by the (already very prosperous) husband of the wealthy local Democrat MP. From further press investigations it was discovered that relatives of other MPs (mostly Democrats but also including members of the opposition) were also benefiting. The deputy minister of Agriculture in charge of the program was eventually forced to resign; and seven of the richest beneficiaries had to

---

[10] *Nakthurakij tekhnokhrat nakkanmuang lae naiphon: khorupchan lae anakhod khong rabob prachathipatai thai* (Businesspeople, technocrats, politicians, and generals: corruption and the future of the Thai democratic system): seminar organized by the Political Economy Centre, Chulalongkorn University, August 1993.

[11] Reported in *The Nation*, April 1, 23, 27, 1993; *Bangkok Post*, December 3, 1993.

give up their titles. The shock to public opinion played a large part in the defection of Palang Dharma, resulting in the collapse of the Chuan government.

MILITARY

The gradual erosion of excessive military powers continued after May 1992; throughout this process, Army Commander-in-Chief Vimol persisted in resisting efforts by politicians to downgrade the military institution, seen as guarantor of Thai security. The Chuan government, too, resisted pressure from the Confederation for Democracy (prominent in the May 1992 protests) and from other elements of civil society to abrogate all military-government decrees and to revoke the amnesty of those involved in the May massacre.

Nevertheless, in March 1993 the Senate confirmed the House's abrogation of the notorious Internal Peacekeeping Directorate Act, which had been invoked to suppress the May 1992 demonstrators. In June 1993 the House approved a bill requiring the approval of Cabinet before troops could be assigned to put down disturbances. The declared unconstitutionality of the military-backed seizure of "assets" was another blow—setting a precedent in regard to further coups.

A sign of the (democratizing) times was the "first of its kind" publication by the Ministry of Defence of a strategic-political analysis in the Western style. *The Defence of Thailand 1994* states that the "Armed Forces conducts its mission in accordance with the Constitution . . ." and that, throughout the world, "a New World Order is emerging with greater emphasis on issues such as democracy, human rights, and environmental conservation. At the same time, the world is entering an information age and there is greater economic competition. All these factors have an effect on our long term planning."

Indeed, the military promotions in 1994 largely favored professional soldiers of the type of Army commander Vimol. During the year, military leaders seldom commented on the government's performance—a striking difference from earlier days. The emergence of the Banharn government, however, brought about two significant changes.

Reproaching the poor reputation of some leading politicians, the army newspaper in August 1995 poured scorn on the new government's "political reform" committee; meanwhile the army radio attacked the prevalence of political corruption, suggesting the possibility (to civilian critics) that the military, as in the old days, was preparing the ground for another coup.

The second change—Defense Minister Chavalit's imposition of his own candidates to head the 1995 promotions list (ignoring Vimol's choice)—opens up quite different perspectives. On the one hand, Chavalit's promotions could be viewed as the results of the democratizing effect of civilian government control of military appointments, as in the West. On the other hand, Chavalit, as a former army commander, could be creating a new power structure combining military and civilian functions in the service of his personal ambition.

Accordingly, former Prime Minister Anand may have been too optimistic when he announced some time before that, even if changes were slow, the military now realized that the days of coups were over. "They cannot go against the trend of public opinion. They cannot go against the global trend which moves towards a market economy and more democratic society." Such is indeed the trend; but between the pressure for greater democratization and a military insisting on its internal independence (from parliamentary scrutiny) there is still ample room for conflict.

LABOR

Although the Chuan government clearly attempted to accommodate labor, raising the minimum wage (for Bangkok from 115 to 125 baht) toward the beginning of 1993 and finally allowing labor unions to be set up in state enterprises (but not to strike) at the end of the year, it did not manage to purchase tranquillity; one of the biggest problems it faced was the strike of textile workers who had been laid off by cost-cutting employers in July 1993. For the issue is far more than a conflict over local labor conditions: it is also a conflict over globalization. On the one hand textile workers, largely women migrating from the provinces, desperately need work under decent conditions; on the other hand, textile companies are facing growing competition from lower-wage countries like Indonesia, and especially China and Vietnam (which are attracting increasing foreign investment).

The July strike dramatically revealed the polarization between workers, indignant at being retrenched without adequate consultation or compensation (in the usual high-handed manner), and employers who came under growing pressure from public opinion—and eventually the government—to end the damaging strike by reinstating the dismissed workers. Despite anxiety not to offend foreign investors, Interior Minister Chavalit ordered the companies to reinstate the workers, and the strike came to an end. Even so, a specialist from the Thailand Development Research Institute argued that factories had to install new equipment to reduce labor costs and improve efficiency if they were to be competitive.

Academics sympathetic to the workers' case also pointed out that Thailand was losing its competitive edge at the lower end of the market; but they emphasized that the government should take greater responsibility in improving work-skills and re-training workers, as well as reforming laws biased against workers. Nikom Chandrivithun, a former director-general of the labor department, pointed out, for example, that less than one third of factories in and around Bangkok paid the minimum wage. Textile workers usually received only 4000 baht a month on average for a sixty-hour week, often under poor conditions. Factory workers were more aware of their rights, he argued, but their unions were weak and disorganized. Under such conditions, the outlook for textile workers was bleak.[12] Nevertheless, wages have improved, especially in the public sector, since 1993; and workers' discontent, although intensely motivated in particular enterprises, remains sporadic and disorganized.

RURAL PROBLEMS

The situation of agriculture is more problematic, as explained in the previous chapter. Thus, the Chuan government, whatever its reformist intentions, inherited official policies that have operated for decades in favor of industrialization and urbanization. In addition, competition for scarce resources, for example between urban speculators (and local Mafia) and poor farmers, has intensified. One result is forest degradation, an environmental dilemma that develops when influential businessmen, on the one hand, and landless peasants, on the other, encroach on ever more limited forest reserves.

Throughout Thailand, farmers whose livelihood depends on the export of crops to world markets are vulnerable to fluctuating demand. Increasingly, they demand

---

[12] Rodney Tasker, "Rendered Surplus," *Far Eastern Economic Review*, July 22, 1993; Chalong-phob Sussangkarn, TDRI [Thai Development Research Institute]; Suthy Prasartset, Faculty of Economics, Chulalongkorn University.

more effective price support measures from the government as well as greater budgetary allocations to the countryside—in particular, for small-scale irrigation projects, feeder roads, agricultural research, and technical help. They also seek protection in the frequent cases of land disputes with the military and with city capitalists, who are often abetted by the provincial authorities.

Alleviation of poverty, especially prevalent in rural areas, and the allocation of increased aid for farmers (suffering lower commodity prices on world markets) were accordingly high among the priorities set by the Chuan government. The government also considered plans to write off more than one billion baht in debts owed by some 200,000 farmers to the state. Nevertheless, despite these accommodations, numerous protests by farmers continue to erupt, which both the Chuan and Banharn governments attempt to mollify—but in a piecemeal fashion.

The Chuan government, for example, issued land-rights titles to more than half a million people in the past two years. But the land tenure of many more is still uncertain, inhibiting improvement, and making it difficult to obtain cheap loans. The land reform scandal in Phuket provides a further example. Even a program free of abuses, as Thongroj Onchan, Dean of Kasetsart's faculty of economics, points out, would hardly benefit those who are most in need: that is, landless or poor farmers who cannot prove their occupation of land.

Significantly, Thongroj argues, neither the Democrat nor Chart Thai leaders have any clear policy on how to deal with such major rural problems as land speculation and forest encroachment. Even well-intentioned political leaders underestimate the power of wealthy influential people, including the local Mafia and provincial politicians, who interfere for their own advantage in agricultural policy decisions, including so-called land reform policies. Thongroj advocates tougher measures, such as a progressive land tax to put pressure on owners to use their land effectively.[13] The Thai Farmers Research Centre also urges more equitable income distribution, facilitated by such actions as the reduction of farm debts, as well as the formation of a National Agricultural Council.

ENVIRONMENT

The Chuan government was increasingly aware of the disastrous consequences of environmental degradation and intended to spend over 22,000 million baht over the next five years attempting to alleviate the problem. Besides the intractable problems of Bangkok (see below) numerous protests were mounted against the harmful effects of official-sponsored power plants and dams, over commercial intrusions into national parks, and because of concern over dangerously low water levels.

Yet, despite clashes over the construction of the Pak Mool dam, the Chuan government refused to stop the controversial construction; nor did it tackle the problem of wasteful use of water resources in the absence of a realistic pricing policy. As for the Mae Moh power plant—another project by the Electricity Generating Authority of Thailand—it had already created one of the biggest pollution scandals in the previous year. Under public pressure, the authority eventually agreed to cut power generation by more than half.

Environmentalists argue that despite the government's good intentions, basic problems largely remain unsolved. In one year, for example, more than a third of popular demonstrations were over environmental issues, especially conflicts over the

---

[13] Thongroj, reported in *Bangkok Post*, June 28, 1995.

use of land, water, and forest resources. Speakers at a seminar on the government's performance argued that too many official agencies were involved and were not properly coordinated. They also asserted that ordinary people had no input into policy-making on the environment.[14]

This situation is unlikely to change for the better under the more commercially-minded ministers of the Banharn government. Agriculture Minister Montri, for example, who favors higher yields from farms, forests, and hydro and electric power, openly disapproves of environmental safeguards that may slow production but also prevent rural degradation.

As the chairman of the Thailand Environment Institute had previously emphasized, until environmental issues are given priority on the political agenda there will be no effective action. He strongly urged greater reduction in the use of fossil fuels (providing more than 80 percent of energy consumption in Thailand) especially in transport, power and industry. He recognized, however, that because of bureaucratic corruption and probable lack of government will to enforce environmental measures, the best way to protect the environment would be through market-based incentives and deterrents, such as emission and fuel taxes.[15]

The capital itself is an environmental nightmare. The economic loss alone (because of congested traffic and polluted air) has been estimated by the World Bank in December 1993 to amount to more than US$3 billion a year. (While the cost of pollution amounts to nearly 10 percent of urban GDP in Asian cities the cost of cleaning up would only be 1 or 2 percent, according to the World Bank.)

Already, some two million private cars travel in Bangkok every day, according to police statistics, clogging the streets. Queen Sirikit had earlier voiced the frustration of citizens exposed to interminable delays—in a city with only about half the proportion of road space per head of comparable cities elsewhere—followed by outspoken criticisms from the king himself in August and September 1995.[16]

Much of the anger and irritation of the people has been vented at the infighting between politicians in the government, dissension which holds up important mass transit projects. Under Chuan, for example, the Democrats and Palang Dharma— electoral rivals for city constituencies—had different responsibilities for the administration of greater Bangkok. Similarly, under Banharn, Palang Dharma and Samak's Prachakorn Thai supervise inner and outer Bangkok, respectively.

Responding to the king's concern, both Thaksin and Samak agreed to work together, the former promising in technocratic style to solve Bangkok's traffic problems within six months. The only way to do so, Thaksin concluded, was to remove private cars from some of Bangkok's streets. Peak associations of industries, hotels, travel agencies and the powerful Thai Bankers' Association agreed on the need to

---

[14] "Environmental problems remain after two years of Chuan government" (in Thai), *Siam Rath sapdavijarn*, January 1–7, 1995; report of seminar on December 22, 1994: see also *Siam Rath sapdavijarn*, January 15–21, 1995. Environmentalists cautioned the Banharn government against going ahead with major dams, as envisioned in Agriculture Ministry proposals, which had not solved flooding and drought in the countryside: *Bangkok Post*, August 30, 1995.

[15] Phaichitr Uathavikul, reported by *Bangkok Post*, December 3, 1993. See also Jonathan Rigg (ed.), *Counting the Costs: Economic Growth and Environmental Change in Thailand* (Singapore: Institute of Southeast Asian Studies, 1996).

[16] See, for example, *Matichon sudsapda*, August 22, 1995.

ban private cars from certain streets, to stagger work hours and introduce a shorter working week.[17]

HEALTH

The Chuan government increased expenditure of 500 million baht for health care and envisaged bringing in eventually more than four million of the "underprivileged" under social security provisions. Among major health problems, drug abuse is said to affect (according to the UN) as many as half a million people in Thailand. Countering the spread of AIDS is also a major concern; professionals and NGO workers have been active in this struggle. A World Bank Report, "Investing in Health," praised the Thai government for its efforts, but noted that already some 600,000 people were HIV infected—a number which could reach four million by the end of the decade. Indeed, the government forecast that AIDS would account for one-third of the deaths of Thai workers by that time, costing as much as US$9 billion. (AIDS strikes people in their most productive years.)

HUMAN RIGHTS—AND THE REGION

Human rights is particularly important to a democratizing government, whose supporters (in May 1992) were among the victims of the then military-dominated regime. Yet, as indicated above, the Chuan government was not prepared to support moves within civil society to bring the perpetrators of violence to justice (they are protected under the provisions of Suchinda's amnesty). The same cautious stance is evident among those who seek a consensus ASEAN view on human rights. "It is natural," Chuan argued at a regional conference in March 1993, "that approaches to the implementation of fundamental human rights vary because of differences in socio-economic, historical, cultural backgrounds, and conditions." Human rights "should evolve at their own pace if they are to be peaceful and sustainable."

The ASEAN "charter" announced in September 1993 further diminished the impact of human rights by insisting that "each member state" has the right to set its own priorities, including the (prior) "right to development." Moreover, support for human rights must be in the context of "respect for national sovereignty, territorial integrity and non-interference in the internal affairs of states"—the standard argument by *states*, which if strictly applied would render the human rights of *citizens* meaningless. (At the previous World Conference on Human Rights at Vienna, the UN Secretary-General had put forward the humanitarian view that when the state fails to guarantee human rights—"when far from being protectors they become tormentors"—then the international community has the right to intercede.)

Eventually, however, something of a compromise was reached. A UN working group approved the (Western-proposed) creation of a Commissioner for Human Rights, able "to engage in dialogue" with governments to secure human rights. In exchange, Third World members of the group agreed not to insist on the priority of economic development over human rights—there is, of course, no reason why they should be mutually exclusive—and to accept that both are necessary.

The test case is Thai relations with countries like Burma, Cambodia, Vietnam, and China, where strategic or economic considerations largely prevail; but not entirely. By 1995, the Chuan and Banharn governments had effectively dissociated themselves from the Khmer Rouge in Cambodia—a situation confirmed by the

---

[17] Reported in *Bangkok Post*, August 24, 1995.

United States—and relations are cooler with the military regime in Burma. Moreover, Thailand has welcomed Vietnam into ASEAN membership.

5

CONCLUSION: DEVELOPMENT AND DEMOCRACY RECONSIDERED

The ambiguities of civil society, described in previous chapters, reflect the wider problematic of "development" and "democracy." Does development basically mean economic growth? Or does it mean growth with equity? And if so, how much "equity" (meaning a more equal distribution of the economic product)? In other words, how much equity can be "afforded" at the expense of growth?

Evidently, the various groups in society have different conceptions of "growth" and "equity" according to their place in the economic system: as large or small owners, as managers or as subordinate staff, as professionals associated with business (corporate lawyers, accountants, architects, engineers) or as independent professionals (teachers, journalists, physicians), as trade union representatives (in the public or private sector) or as workers (male or female, organized or informal), as village leaders and, finally, as consumers. Each has a different interest and a different conception of what development means or should mean.

But how can these conceptions be *realized*? This depends, not only on a person's relation to the economy, but also on the type of political system (whether authoritarian or pluralistic) and the open or restrictive character of society. Differing conceptions then emerge as part of a process of legitimation or identification, on the one hand, and indifference or rejection, on the other. Thus, in regard to the economic system, "capitalism" has a different meaning for owners, managers, or workers, who might variously approve of it, entertain suspicions against it, or reject it. In terms of the political system, the meaning of the concept of "nation" fluctuates likewise; and similarly for "democracy."

To take the first case: if development ("capitalism") is understood and widely accepted as the natural operation of market forces, healthy competition, and level playing fields, resulting in economic growth and consumer comforts, then members of capitalist society think and behave in the appropriate manner. But if development is understood—and criticized or rejected—as the exploitation of the powerless, through the appropriation of the social product by a powerful and wealthy elite, resulting in misery and conflict, then people think and act very differently.

Similarly in regard to nationalism.[1] The phrase, "Nation, religion, monarchy," for example, was originally coined by King Vajiravudh to demonstrate national

---

[1] "Nationalism" and "nationality," as Benedict Anderson points out, are "cultural artifacts of a particular kind" that have emerged historically and changed their meanings over time: *Imagined Communities: Reflections on the Origins and Spread of Nationalism* (London: Verso, 1983), pp. 14–19, 28.

solidarity—a new concept—under "absolute monarchy." Half a century later, the watchword "nation" was appropriated by the dictator, Marshal Sarit, as a way of legitimizing "national development" under military rule. At the present stage of economic and political development, "nation, religion, monarchy" is intended to justify what the critics call "semi-democracy": that is, representative forms of government compromised by the authoritarian tendencies of the bureaucracy and the overpowering interests of business. In other words, "democracy in the Thai style."

Just as nationalism was identified with state power, under the bureaucratic polity, and is now identified with an informal partnership between political and economic elites, so "democracy" also means different things to different people.[2] On the right, the military appropriates the formula of "democracy in the Thai style" in an attempt to uphold the status quo. Military leaders see themselves as "guardians" of the three sacred institutions (nation, religion, monarchy) in the belief that whatever is contrary to military interests is a threat to democracy—Thai style. Conversely, the middle class interprets these "institutions," generally in a conservative way, to mean the "nation" of business, the religion of "individualistic" Buddhism, and the monarchy that is revered because it is "above" politics. Reformers and idealists in turn emphasize the democratic potential of the "people-nation," progressive Buddhism, and constitutional monarchy.

Such a process of differentiation occurs not only within a country—spatially— but also historically. In nineteenth century Britain, for example, democracy (identified with "mob rule") was quite unacceptable to a parliament that was dominated first by the aristocracy and then by the middle class. It was not until toward the end of the century that democracy could be acknowledged: by this time the "masses," previously considered to be dangerously unruly and ignorant, were deemed to have become "respectable" (that is to say, domesticated) in the eyes of the upper classes.

This process is now under way in the "developing" world. In Latin America, but also to an extent in East and Southeast Asia, military dictators have transferred power to civilians, first because the military had proved incapable of resolving highly destabilizing economic or social crises and, second, because a mature, "responsible" civil society had emerged. The result is a democracy that wields power "safely" by facilitating economic growth and by eschewing drastic action against the military institution. It is this interpretation of democracy (or "semi-democracy") as a "safe" arrangement that is, in turn, being contested by a new generation of reformers and radicals.

There is, however, one major difference between the two worlds. Historically, in the West, the political rights of citizens (celebrated in both the American and the French Revolutions) were proclaimed prior to the ascendancy of industrial capitalism. It was only as capitalism developed that the notion of political rights flowed

---

[2] "The spread of democracy became ipso facto a cross-cultural, cross-language phenomenon, involving essentially a complex and ongoing process of signification, translation and interpretation whereby 'democracy' left one semantic field and entered another. . . ." This cross-cultural, cross-language landing of democracy caused it to "disintegrate into free-floating signifiers (the word 'democracy'), multiple signifieds (the notions of democracy) and substitute referents (the 'democratic' thing).": Kasian Tejapira, "Signification of Democracy," paper for workshop on "Comparative Perceptions of Democracy and Government," Brisbane, November 1992. This tendency to plurality of meanings and usages is evident in other semantic cultural borrowings, such as the terms "rights," "legitimacy," and "the people," which are an integral part of the democratic conception: Diana Wong (referring to research by Reinhart Kosellek), workshop on democratization, Institute of Southeast Asian Studies, October 1993.

over into economic rights: for example, the legal status of corporate bodies considered as individual persons. This process corresponded to the change from mercantilism (the subordination of economic resources to state power) to a market economy.

In East and Southeast Asia, to the contrary, this historic transformation has been reversed. "Economic rights"—especially in the "private sector"—come first, reflecting the priority given to capitalist development. Nevertheless, as the economy expands, it creates the preconditions for civil society—and, with it, pressures for democracy. It is then that economic rights flow on to the demand for political rights.

It is the ascendant middle class, however, that increasingly "represents" this constitutional process, appropriating political rights just as it appropriated economic rights. "Development" is the hegemonic ideology of the middle class, taking various forms: economic, where it signifies unfettered growth; political, where it has to do with parliamentary order; and cultural, where it posits the value of materialism, pragmatism, individualism. The middle class in Thailand is the wave of the future; but unlike Huntington's "third wave" (see the first chapter), it may not necessarily bring with it a liberal-democratic, and still less a social-democratic, future.

To sum up: there are three great spheres of social existence—the economic, the political, and the civil sphere. In Thailand, capitalist development is the most dynamic, with the potential to increase Thai national wealth to the level of present-day South Korea or Taiwan; but this is skewed development, Bangkok-based, and it increases the gap between rich and poor. The political means exist—in the state and the "democratizing" institutions—both to facilitate capitalist development and, redistributively, to redress its inequities; but a bureaucracy determined to preserve its authority and politicians determined to enhance their power and wealth impede the country's advancement toward more equitable distribution of resources, opportunities, and civil liberties. Each of these groups dictates different priorities. It is left to civil society to speak out for the interests of ordinary people.

Non-governmental organizations, in particular, represent the *spontaneous* strength of the nation-people striving for a more just society (demonstrated especially at times of crisis); but they cannot—from lack of power and wealth—make this strength permanent. For this they need the *institutional* resources of a (reformed) party and parliamentary system. It is only in this way, with the symbiosis of civil society and political organization, that order and justice can be achieved.

SOUTHEAST ASIA PROGRAM PUBLICATIONS
Cornell University

Studies on Southeast Asia

Number 1 *The Symbolism of the Stupa,* Adrian Snodgrass. 1985. Reprinted with index, 1988. 2nd printing, 1991. 469 pp. ISBN 0-87727-700-1

Number 3 *Thai Radical Discourse: The Real Face of Thai Feudalism Today,* Craig J. Reynolds. 1987. 2nd printing 1994. 186 pp. ISBN 0-87727-702-8

Number 5 *Southeast Asian Ephemeris: Solar and Planetary Positions, A.D. 638–2000,* J. C. Eade. 1989. 175 pp. ISBN 0-87727-704-4

Number 6 *Trends in Khmer Art,* Jean Boisselier. Ed. Natasha Eilenberg. Trans. Natasha Eilenberg and Melvin Elliott. 1989. 124 pp., 24 plates. ISBN 0-87727-705-2

Number 7 *A Malay Frontier: Unity and Duality in a Sumatran Kingdom,* Jane Drakard. 1990. 215 pp. ISBN 0-87727-706-0

Number 8 *The Politics of Colonial Exploitation: Java, the Dutch, and the Cultivation System,* Cornelis Fasseur. Ed. R. E. Elson. Trans. R. E. Elson and Ary Kraal. 1992. 2nd printing 1994. 266 pp. ISBN 0-87727-707-9

Number 9 *Southeast Asian Capitalists,* ed. Ruth McVey. 1992. 220 pp. ISBN 0-87727-708-7

Number 10 *Tai Ahoms and the Stars: Three Ritual Texts to Ward Off Danger,* trans. and ed. B. J. Terwiel and Ranoo Wichasin. 1992. 170 pp. ISBN 0-87727-709-5

Number 11 *Money, Markets, and Trade in Early Southeast Asia: The Development of Indigenous Monetary Systems to AD 1400,* Robert S. Wicks. 1992. 354 pp., 78 tables, illus., maps. ISBN 0-87727-710-9

Number 12 *Fields from the Sea: Chinese Junk Trade with Siam during the Late Eighteenth and Early Nineteenth Centuries,* Jennifer Cushman. 1993. 214 pp. ISBN 0-87727-711-7

Number 13 *Fair Land Sarawak: Some Recollections of an Expatriate Officer,* Alastair Morrison. 1993. 196 pp. ISBN 0-87727-712-5

Number 14 *Sjahrir: Politics and Exile in Indonesia,* Rudolf Mrázek. 1994. 536 pp. ISBN 0-87727-713-3

Number 15 *Selective Judicial Competence: The Cirebon-Priangan Legal Administration, 1680–1792,* Mason C. Hoadley. 1994. 185 pp. ISBN 0-87727-714-1

Number 16 *The Nan Chronicle,* trans. and ed. by David K. Wyatt. 1994. 158 pp. ISBN 0-87727-715-X

Number 17 *The Vernacular Press and the Emergence of Modern Indonesian Consciousness,* Ahmat Adam. 1995. 220 pp. ISBN 0-87727-716-8

Number 18 *In the Land of Lady White Blood: Southern Thailand and the Meaning of History,* Lorraine M. Gesick. 1995. 106 pp. ISBN 0-87727-717-6

Number 19 *Essays into Vietnamese Pasts,* ed. K. W. Taylor and John K. Whitmore. 1995. 288 pp. ISBN 0-87727-718-4

Number 20 *Making Indonesia,* ed. Daniel S. Lev and Ruth McVey. 1996. 201 pp. ISBN 0-87727-719-2

Number 21 *Interpreting Development: Capitalism, Democracy, and the Middle Class in Thailand,* John Girling. 1996. 95 pp. ISBN 0-87727-720-6

SEAP Series

Number 2   *The Dobama Movement in Burma (1930–1938)*, Khin Yi. 1988. 160 pp. ISBN 0-87727-118-6

Number 3   *Postwar Vietnam: Dilemmas in Socialist Development*, ed. Christine White and David Marr. 1988. 2nd printing, 1993. 260 pp. ISBN 0-87727-120-8

Number 5   *Japanese Relations with Vietnam: 1951–1987*, Masaya Shiraishi. 1990. 174 pp. ISBN 0-87727-122-4

Number 6   *The Rise and Fall of the Communist Party of Burma (CPB)*, Bertil Lintner. 1990. 124 pp. 26 plates, 14 maps. ISBN 0-87727-123-2

Number 7   *Intellectual Property and US Relations with Indonesia, Malaysia, Singapore, and Thailand*, Elisabeth Uphoff. 1991. 67 pp. ISBN 0-87727-124-0

Number 8   *From PKI to the Comintern, 1924–1941: The Apprenticeship of the Malayan Communist Party*, Cheah Boon Kheng. 1992. 147 pp. ISBN 0-87727-125-9

Number 9   *A Secret Past*, Dokmaisot. Trans. Ted Strehlow. 1992. 72 pp. ISBN 0-87727-126-7

Number 10   *Studies on Vietnamese Language and Literature: A Preliminary Bibliography*, Nguyen Dinh Tham. 1992. 227 pp. ISBN 0-87727-127-5

Number 11   *The Political Legacy of Aung San*, ed. Josef Silverstein. 1972, rev. ed. 1993. 169 pp. ISBN 0-87727-128-3

Number 12   *The Voice of Young Burma*, Aye Kyaw. 1993. 98 pp. ISBN 0-87727-129-1

Number 13   *The American War in Vietnam*, ed. Jayne Werner & David Hunt. 1993. 132 pp. ISBN 0-87727-131-3

Number 14   *Being Kammu: My Village, My Life*, ed. Damrong Tayanin. 1994. 138 pp. ISBN 0-87727-130-5

Number 15   *The Revolution Falters: The Left in Philippine Politics After 1986.* ed. Patricio N. Abinales. 1996. 183 pp. ISBN 0-87727-132-1

Translation Series

Volume 1   *Reading Southeast Asia*, ed. Takashi Shiraishi. 1990. 188 pp. ISBN 0-87727-400-2

Volume 2   *Indochina in the 1940s and 1950s*, ed. Takashi Shiraishi & Motoo Furuta. 1992. 196 pp. ISBN 0-87727-401-0

Volume 3   *The Japanese in Colonial Southeast Asia*, ed. Saya Shiraishi & Takashi Shiraishi. 1993. 172 pp. ISBN 0-87727-402-9

Volume 4   *Approaching Suharto's Indonesia from the Margins*, ed. Takashi Shiraishi. 1994. 153 pp. ISBN 0-87727-403-7

Number 6 *The Indonesian Elections of 1955*, Herbert Feith. 1957. 2d printing, 1971. 91 pp. ISBN 0-87763-020-8

Number 7 *The Soviet View of the Indonesian Revolution*, Ruth T. McVey. 1957. 3d printing, 1969. 90 pp. ISBN 0-87763-018-6

Number 25 *The Communist Uprisings of 1926–1927 in Indonesia: Key Documents*, ed. and intro. Harry J. Benda and Ruth T. McVey. 1960. 2d printing, 1969. 177 pp. ISBN 0-87763-024-0

Number 37 *Mythology and the Tolerance of the Javanese*, Benedict R. Anderson. 1965. 6th printing, 1988. 77 pp. ISBN 0-87763-023-2

Number 43 *State and Statecraft in Old Java: A Study of the Later Mataram Period, 16th to 19th Century*, Soemarsaid Moertono. 1968. Rev. ed., 1981. 180 pp. ISBN 0-87763-017-8

Number 48 *Nationalism, Islam and Marxism*, Soekarno. Intro. by Ruth T. McVey. 1970. 2d printing, 1984. 62 pp. ISBN 0-87763-012-7

Number 49 *The Foundation of the Partai Muslimin Indonesia*, K. E. Ward. 1970. 75 pp. ISBN 0-87763-011-9

Number 50 *Schools and Politics: The Kaum Muda Movement in West Sumatra (1927–1933)*, Taufik Abdullah. 1971. 257 pp. ISBN 0-87763-010-0

Number 51 *The Putera Reports: Problems in Indonesian-Javanese War-Time Cooperation*, Mohammad Hatta. Trans. and intro. William H. Frederick. 1971. 114 pp. ISBN 0-87763-009-7

Number 52 *A Preliminary Analysis of the October 1, 1965, Coup in Indonesia* (Prepared in January 1966), Benedict R. Anderson, Ruth T. McVey, assist. Frederick P. Bunnell. 1971. 174 pp. ISBN 0-87763-008-9

Number 55 *Report from Banaran: The Story of the Experiences of a Soldier during the War of Independence*, Maj. Gen. T. B. Simatupang. 1972. 186 pp. ISBN 0-87763-005-4

Number 57 *Permesta: Half a Rebellion*, Barbara S. Harvey. 1977. 174 pp. ISBN 0-87763-033-8

Number 58 *Administration of Islam in Indonesia*, Deliar Noer. 1978. 82 pp. ISBN 0-87763-002-X

Number 59 *Breaking the Chains of Oppression of the Indonesian People: Defense Statement at His Trial on Charges of Insulting the Head of State, Bandung, June 7–10, 1979*, Heri Akhmadi. 1981. 201 pp. ISBN 0-87763-001-1

Number 60 *The Minangkabau Response to Dutch Colonial Rule in the Nineteenth Century*, Elizabeth E. Graves. 1981. 157 pp. ISBN 0-87763-000-3

Number 61 *Sickle and Crescent: The Communist Revolt of 1926 in Banten*, Michael C. Williams. 1982. 81 pp. ISBN 0-87763-027-5

Number 62 *Interpreting Indonesian Politics: Thirteen Contributions to the Debate, 1964–1981*. Ed. Benedict Anderson and Audrey Kahin, intro. Daniel S. Lev. 1982. 3rd printing 1991. 172 pp. ISBN 0-87763-028-3

Number 64 *Suharto and His Generals: Indonesia's Military Politics, 1975–1983*, David Jenkins. 1984. 3rd printing 1987. 300 pp. ISBN 0-87763-027-5

Number 65 *The Kenpeitai in Java and Sumatra.* Trans. from the Japanese by Barbara G. Shimer and Guy Hobbs, intro. Theodore Friend. 1986. 80 pp. ISBN 0-87763-031-3

Number 66 *Prisoners at Kota Cane,* Leon Salim. Trans. Audrey Kahin. 1986. 112 pp. ISBN 0-87763-032-1

Number 67 *Indonesia Free: A Biography of Mohammad Hatta,* Mavis Rose. 1987. 252 pp. ISBN 0-87763-033-X

Number 68 *Intellectuals and Nationalism in Indonesia: A Study of the Following Recruited by Sutan Sjahrir in Occupation Jakarta,* J. D. Legge. 1988. 159 pp. ISBN 0-87763-034-8

Number 69 *The Road to Madiun: The Indonesian Communist Uprising of 1948,* Elizabeth Ann Swift. 1989. 120 pp. ISBN 0-87763-035-6

Number 70 *East Kalimantan: The Decline of a Commercial Aristocracy,* Burhan Magenda. 1991. 120 pp. ISBN 0-87763-036-4

Number 71 *A Japanese Memoir of Sumatra, 1945–1946: Love and Hatred in the Liberation War,* Takao Fusayama. 1993. 150 pp. ISBN 0-87763-037-2

Number 72 *Popular Indonesian Literature of the Qur'an,* Howard M. Federspiel. 1994. 170 pp. ISBN 0-87763-038-0

Number 73 *"White Book" on the 1992 General Election in Indonesia,* Trans. Dwight King. 1994. 72 pp. ISBN 0-87763-039-9

Number 74 *The Roots of Acehnese Rebellion 1989–1992,* Tim Kell. 1995. 103 pp. ISBN 0-87727-040-2

* * *

Javanese Literature in Surakarta Manuscripts, Nancy K. Florida. Hardcover series ISBN 0-87727-600-5; Paperback series ISBN 0-87727-601-3. Vol. 1, *Introduction and Manuscripts of the Karaton Surakarta.* 1993. 410 pp. Frontispiece and 5 illus. Hardcover, ISBN 0-87727-602-1, Paperback, ISBN 0-87727-603-X

Sbek Thom: Khmer Shadow Theater. ed. Thavro Phim & Sos Kem. 1996. 363 pp., incl. 153 photographs. ISBN 0-87727-620-X.

In the Mirror, Literature and Politics in Siam in the American Era, ed. and trans. Benedict R. Anderson and Ruchira Mendiones. 1985. 2nd printing, 1991. 303 pp. Paperback. ISBN 974-210-380-1

For ordering information, please contact:

Southeast Asia Program Publications
Distribution/Purchase Orders
Cornell University
East Hill Plaza
Ithaca, NY 14850

Telephone: (607) 255-8038
Fax: (607) 277-1904